Advance Praise for *The Winning Formula*

'This [book] is not about being superhuman; [it] is about realising that being human is super'

Sadhguru

'[This] book will be a source of inspiration to the coming generation'

Shiv Khera, motivational speaker and author

'This heartwarming book contains fifty-two magical chapters. Together they encompass maxims for a well-lived life. On the one hand, it is a collection of manifestations to help us attain our life goals with intentional, conscious thought, and on the other, it captures the everyday heroism of people who overcome limitations of circumstances to make this world a little better, every day in every way … sterling gems and everyday heroes honourably recorded in this heartfelt endeavour. This book is a must-read'

Amish, author

'*The Winning Formula* … is unique in a lot of aspects. Unlike many motivational books, this book is not theoretical. There are … incredibly touching tales … of regular people accomplishing impactful things. I think this is a book that everyone should read, regardless of age. It will significantly alter their lives'

P.S. Sreedharan Pillai, Governor of Goa

'*The Winning Formula* is an insightful read with rare brilliance in its content and presentation … The book equips the new generation with all the tools with which they can rush like a bull through any thicket of thorns when they face the test of life and examinations. This book is to be tasted, swallowed, chewed and digested … An excellent book from an excellent mind which spurs the reader on to the pursuit of excellence'

Dr C.V. Ananda Bose, Governor of West Bengal

'K.J. Alphons's life story spans many domains – civil servant, politician and above all a thought leader. It is the search for excellence that defines his approach to life, but excellence that serves the wider circle of humanity. *The Winning Formula* is the inspiring story of his journey through an eventful life and the inspirational stories of many other individuals who share his philosophy and thinking and have achieved outstanding success in their endeavours. This is a book which will remain relevant for many years to come and shine a pathway for our aspirational youth'

Shyam Saran, former Foreign Secretary

'Alphons … writes straight from the heart in a lucid, simple style that would appeal to every reader. The book can easily be read at one go, so engaging is his manner of writing. An excellent contribution, particularly useful to the young seeking to build their own lives'

K.M. Chandrasekhar, former Cabinet Secretary

'The book will provide inspiration for the younger generation, but the message is that perspiration is also essential for success'

T.P. Sreenivasan, former ambassador

'Alphons … has ably prescribed a weekly dosage of oxygen … It is possible to achieve success and happiness if you follow the prescription'

H.K. Dua, former ambassador, media adviser to the Prime Minister and former editor, *Hindustan Times*, *The Indian Express* and *The Tribune*

'K.J. Alphons draws from his extraordinary journey as an IAS officer, politician and advocate to offer profound life lessons that can inspire anyone to achieve greatness. With decades of public service under his belt, Alphons offers insights that are not only motivational but deeply rooted in the first-hand experiences of dynamic leaders in today's fast-paced world. This book serves as a powerful cultivator of self-belief. Reminding us that ordinary people can achieve extraordinary things – and that we are, in any given moment, just one step away from greatness. This book will ignite that spark, guiding you to conquer and lead a life of purpose'

Amitabh Kant, G20 Sherpa, former CEO, NITI Aayog, and author

'This is a book of insights drawn from a life well lived and from the lives of those who went the extra mile. In his easy-to-read style, Alphons writes of fifty-two lessons – one for each week of the year – that he learnt from his own experience, the people he met and the books he read over a long and eventful career as a student, civil servant and finally a politician. Read it, mull over it and occasionally smile'

Sanjeev Sanyal, member of the Economic Advisory Council to the Prime Minister of India and author

'[An] eminently readable and relatable book ... The message is loud and clear: one does not have to be born with a silver spoon or endowed with extraordinary skills to initiate change. All it requires is determination, a positive outlook and the willingness to take the plunge'

Dr Sanjeev Chopra, former director, Lal Bahadur Shastri National Academy of Administration

'This book is an emphatic testament to the belief that one can recast one's life by merely choosing to act, no matter their background. The author's journey of personal development, resilience and success ... provides the stimulus and means for anyone to uncover their potential to attain excellence'

Mamidala Jagadesh Kumar, chairperson, University Grants Commission, and former vice chancellor, Jawaharlal Nehru University

'In this one-of-a-kind book ... K.J. Alphons adorns a new role in his illustrious public career – life coach, motivational speaker and author. Drawing from the wealth of wisdom amassed from years of public service, he has masterfully captured the story of his life and the lives of some remarkable individuals, presenting them with a sense of simplicity and universality that resonates with readers of all ages. If one commits to reading and reflecting on one story and its message each week for the next fifty-two weeks, this book holds the potential to transform lives'

Prof. (Dr) C. Raj Kumar, founding vice chancellor,
O.P. Jindal Global University, and
dean, Jindal Global Law School

'[A] blueprint for transformation of one's life. It is insightful and a must-read'

Rahul Singh, chairperson, Central Board of
Secondary Education

'*The Winning Formula* is a powerful roadmap for personal transformation and success. With practical insights drawn from his own life experiences, he provides actionable strategies that can inspire anyone to make meaningful changes. This book is a compelling guide for anyone aspiring to turn challenges into opportunities and achieve their fullest potential. I would recommend all school and college students, their parents and teachers to read the book'

Dr Joseph Emmanuel, chief executive and secretary,
Council for the Indian School Certificate Examinations

'In their simplicity, Alphons's stories perform one task rather beautifully: they tell you that no wall that one comes across in life is insurmountable. For that feat alone, the book is highly recommended'

Rahul Pandita, author

The Winning Formula

The Winning Formula

52 Ways to Change Your Life

K.J. ALPHONS

BLOOMSBURY
NEW DELHI • LONDON • OXFORD • NEW YORK • SYDNEY

than I did. Lot of people don't believe in their abilities. You just have to believe in yourself and your destiny. Dream the big dream. You have to work hard to make those dreams a reality.' Throughout *The Winning Formula*, Alphons exalts numerous ordinary Indians whose heroic deeds made them extraordinary, urging us to follow their example. If he includes himself among their ranks – and, have no doubt about it, he very much belongs there – he does so not to toot his own horn but to crystallise the ideals he seeks to instil in us, for as he writes: 'There are autobiographical elements in this book as I thought it would be easier for you to relate to my life …'

What a commendable range of lessons – fifty-two of them, one for each week of the year – Alphons has chosen to impart in *The Winning Formula*! So this volume runs the gamut from what changes we can make in our lifestyles to counteract climate change (in 'Jadav Payeng: A Beacon of Hope for the Planet') to how thinking outside the box (in 'With Them They Brought Light') is at times the only way forward. Drawing on both his memory and the headlines, Alphons sheds much-needed light on the lives of some sadly unknown Indians who, hailing from different parts of the country and disparate socioeconomic backgrounds, rose to serve their country and their compatriots, spreading love and laughter beyond the superficial barriers of religion and language, and, in so doing, served the cause of a peaceful and progressive India.

Sometimes playful, sometimes poignant, instructive and illuminating, K.J. Alphons's *The Winning Formula: 52 Ways to Change Your Life* is bound to make you reflect on your thoughts and actions, and learn and unlearn in equal measure, paving the way to an *inspired* life which, in due course, will empower you to lead an *inspiring* life. For this we are much beholden to the author – though I suspect that he will consider himself amply rewarded if we seriously

BLOOMSBURY INDIA
Bloomsbury Publishing India Pvt. Ltd
Second Floor, LSC Building No. 4, DDA Complex, Pocket C – 6 & 7,
Vasant Kunj, New Delhi, 110070

BLOOMSBURY, BLOOMSBURY INDIA and the Diana logo
are trademarks of Bloomsbury Publishing Plc

First published in India 2024
This edition published 2024

ISBN: PB: 978-93-56408-60-9; eBook: 978-93-56409-46-0
2 4 6 8 10 9 7 5 3

Typeset in Adobe Garamond by Manipal Technologies Limited
Printed and bound in India by Gopsons Papers Pvt. Ltd., Noida

MIX
Paper | Supporting responsible forestry
FSC® C191020
www.fsc.org

Contents

To my grandchildren Shiva and Sai
May the joy of life and curiosity for its wonders
lead you to paths less travelled

Foreword

In *The Winning Formula: 52 Ways to Change Your Life*, K.J. Alphons upends Søren Kierkegaard's universally accepted maxim that life is lived forwards, but understood backwards. Reminding us throughout that we 'are just one step away from being extraordinary', and that prodigiousness is an attainable quality, Alphons encourages us to foster a formidable will. For if the sails of our life's ship are propelled by the winds of resolve, we can chart out the entire course of our existence, all while striving on and on, our arms outstretched towards our loftiest dreams. Only when we lapse into complacency, Alphons seems to argue, when we are unwilling to step out of our comfort zone, are we constrained, as the Danish existentialist put it, to understand life backwards. But if we are willing to challenge ourselves, wage a battle against our own indolence and ignorance, then we are apt to succeed and soar – as Alphons has, throughout his life.

Alphons's has been a fascinating life, and fascinatingly does he narrate it. His is a saga to which not only every aspirational youngster and ambitious adult, but every spirited child, will relate. After all, here is a man who rose from being an indifferent school student – who scored a derisory 42 per cent in his class 10 board examinations – to one of the toppers of the immensely competitive Indian Administrative Service examinations in 1979, thus becoming a jewel in India's governmental crown. From here there was no going back: an impressive career in the IAS followed, first as the district collector of Kottayam, which became under his stewardship the first town in India to achieve 100 per cent literacy; and later as the commissioner of the Delhi Development Authority, during which stint, as he vigorously sought to crack down on illegal constructions and organised crime, his family lived in the shadow of threats, all because Alphons showed the courage to effect meaningful change.

At fifty-two, realising that through politics one can herald revolutionary changes, Alphons resigned as the land revenue commissioner of Kerala and leapt into the turbulence of electoral politics – and, upon contesting an assembly election as an independent candidate with the backing of the Left Front, won at his first attempt. The trail he now began to blaze, which won him a best MLA award in 2009, whetted his urge to serve his fellow Indians (and not just fellow Keralites) on a larger scale. This catapulted him to the BJP and to New Delhi; here, in 2017, he became a union minister, with independent charge, of tourism, as also the minister of state for information technology and electronics, for three years. Losing those positions was something he took in stride. 'I believe that humility has to be at the core of a politician's character,' he writes while reflecting on his journey, 'as the people have elected me to be their representative. It is a humbling experience. When God and the citizen entrust me with power and authority, how could I not be humble?' I could not agree more. There can be no greater satisfaction than knowing, when you go to bed at night, that you have served your country well. And this is the satisfaction that Alphons has known.

Yet at no point in *The Winning Formula* is Alphons boastful – or preachy. Of hubris there is no trace in this book; indeed, Alphons writes in the Preface that he is writing this book not to tell us that he is exceptional, but to convince us that he is *not*. 'Yes,' he says, 'I have done things others considered impossible.' But then he immediately adds: 'Whatever I have done with my life, you can do it better engage with this enriching work, seeking to imbibe the ideals he outlines. Read on!

Shashi Tharoor
Member of Parliament and author

Foreword

I am very happy that my good friend K.J. Alphons has taken pains to script the success story of himself and of some he came across in his journey.

'A successful man is one who can lay a firm foundation with the bricks others have thrown at him,' said David Brinkley. Alphons has beautifully captured his journey from a small village to the heights of recognition as a civil servant, elected member of the Legislative Assembly, parliamentarian, union minister and presently a renowned lawyer and arbitrator. His journey exemplifies the transformative potential that lies within each of us. His compelling narrative is not just a personal account, it is a clarion call for anyone who has ever felt overshadowed by circumstances or limited by self-doubt. This book is a testament to the idea that change begins with a single decision – a choice to challenge the status quo and to believe in one's potential. As he shares his story alongside those of many other remarkable individuals, the distinguished author invites readers to see that greatness can emerge from the most humble beginnings, which is the core theme of the book.

This book is more than a collection of inspirational tales; it is a roadmap for personal and professional growth. Alphons offers invaluable insights drawn from his diverse experiences, making it an essential read for people of all ages and backgrounds. Whether you are a student, a professional or someone seeking a new direction in life, you will find motivation and guidance in these pages, if not a true challenge. The author's commitment to paying back to society by igniting change in others is evident in his thoughtful approach, encouraging readers to reflect on each idea, digest it and apply it to their own lives – an invitation to embark on a transformative journey.

'Sprouted in fire, will not wither away in the sun' is a famous saying in Malayalam. In my opinion, the author is challenging the current generation to embrace hardships, persevere through the rough tides and emerge skilful sailors, like the author himself and the many inspiring lives portrayed in the book. Hearty congratulations to dear Alphons for his great efforts and wish the book, the author, the publishers and the myriad readers all the success. God bless.

Justice Kurian Joseph
Former Judge, Supreme Court of India

Preface

There is one small act by which the ordinary can turn extraordinary. It involves standing up and saying: I have to change the status quo. It's like a switch. Once you turn it on, you can row your boat against the strongest of tides.

One day I made up my mind and that was it. From there, every day became exciting; every day was a new experience. I wrote this book to tell you about my life's transformation and what it has accomplished. Along with my own, I also tell stories of thirty-nine other individuals who, like me, decided to press that switch. I hope they can inspire you. I hope they can provide you with the little fuel you need to embark upon your journey of change. Remember, you are just one step away from being extraordinary. This book can change your life dramatically.

I am the son of a schoolteacher, about whom nobody has heard of outside my village. He joined the British army during the Second World War as he hated Hitler and also had the hope that, with India cooperating with Great Britain during the war, India would be granted independence soon after the war. He fought the Second World War as a foot soldier and was at the famous battle of Kohima, where most of his colleagues died fighting the Japanese in a fierce, decisive battle, in which the Japanese were repulsed. He survived. He was still a bachelor. After the war he deserted the British army in 1946, as Great Britain refused to grant independence to India. Churchill hated India and Attlee was not in a hurry. As the British army came after my father for deserting the army, he took refuge in Sathara, a small town in Maharashtra. He got a decent job as he was fluent in English. He got married and had three children before the family relocated to their ancestral village, Manimala, in Kottayam district, where I was born. My father became a teacher in the local school; he taught history and English. Eventually, my parents had nine children. They adopted two children and we became eleven. My village didn't have electricity; we studied under the kerosene lamp. We lived in a 5-acre farm; all of us children worked with the farmhands and ate at the same table. We had enough food to eat, clothes to wear, and we had fun. That was luxury enough. We lacked nothing. We were happy as kids.

I was a hugely underperforming child in school. I never won a prize. In the decisive tenth board examinations, I got 42 per cent. Everybody said that I had no brains and no talents.

One fine day I decided that I had brains and talents. In the university, I won almost every prize. I was one of the toppers of the Indian Administrative Service examinations in 1979. I pioneered many path-breaking initiatives. I won the Best District Collector award multiple times. I knocked down 14,310 illegal buildings belonging to the mafia in India's capital, Delhi. I carried a gun for eight years. My wife went to the market under police protection. Still, she got beaten up trying to clean garbage on the streets of Delhi during the plague outbreak in the mid-1990s. My children went to school under police protection.

I was in *Time* magazine's list of '100 Young Global Leaders' in 1994. There were two of us from India in the list. I quit IAS at fifty-two and got elected to the Kerala State Legislative Assembly, as an independent candidate, thirty-two days later. I completely redefined what an MLA could be. I won the best MLA award. I quit the Kerala Legislative Assembly the day I was renominated to recontest in 2011 and moved to Delhi to join national politics.

I became the union minister of tourism, with independent charge, in 2017. I became a member of Parliament (MP) from Rajasthan, one of the most culturally rich states in India. As an MP, I delivered hugely impactful speeches on the economy, education and healthcare. I retired from Parliament in 2022, and I am opening a new chapter in my book of life. I have no clue what would be in that chapter. I am sure that there are a lot of interesting things I can experiment with at seventy.

You might think that I am exceptional. I am writing this book to tell you that I am not. Yes, I have done things others considered impossible. Whatever I have done with my life, you can do it better than I did. A lot of people don't believe in their abilities. You just have to believe in yourself and your destiny. Dream the big dream. You have to work hard to make those dreams a reality. Nobody has died of hard work; people die of boredom.

There are autographical elements in this book as I thought it would be easier for you to relate to my life than to the great heroes of history; I am an ordinary man with a long list of failures and resurrections. I have also written about other ordinary people who have done extraordinary things, people whom I admire greatly.

Who should read this book? These stories are for all age groups. It can inspire even a primary school kid. Parents, please read it to them. These stories can energise the motivations of teenagers. Just sacrifice one pizza to buy this book. For a young professional venturing into the world, this book talks about the unlimited possibilities the world opens for them. For bureaucrats and corporate leaders who are interested in delivering results, this could be a textbook. For the retired, it tells you how to lead meaningful and content lives.

This book contains a thought for a week for fifty-two weeks. Initially, I wanted to give you an idea a day, 365 ideas for 365 days. Then I realised that you need time to munch and digest an idea and get cracking. A week is long enough to do that; one day is not enough. I suggest that you do not read more than one chapter a week. Take ten minutes every evening to reflect on the thought at the end of each chapter for a week and internalise how you are going to transform your life based on that thought. Put down your decisions on the notepad of your mobile. If you are the writing type, put it down in a diary. If you do that for fifty-two weeks, you will transform your life.

Though the stories in this book have an Indian context, the underlying principles are universal. Readers anywhere in the world will be able to relate to them.

Go, conquer the world. An ordinary man like me did it. You are not ordinary. You will do it a million times better.

1

The Disaster and the Take-Off

The Disaster

When I was three years old, I was packed off to my grandparents' house to be brought up by them. It was a common practice to send off children to grandparents. No one pampers you like them.

Since I was a frail kid, my grandparents decided that it would be unwise to send me to a regular school as I would not be able to stand up to the school bullies. Though frail, I was a very mischievous kid. I was homeschooled by a tutor, called an 'ashan', till I was enrolled in class 3 in Erathuvadakara Lower Primary School, hardly 500 metres from the ancestral home. Of course, it was a Malayalam-medium school. The school had just five classrooms, one room each for classes one to five. I was a front bencher throughout my school days as I was always the tiniest. The school was on the banks of the Manimala river, as was my house. I learnt swimming when I was five. It was a life skill we all picked up early.

I did nothing remarkable while I was in the Eradathuvadakara school. Then I moved to the school my father taught at for classes 6 and 7. After that I moved to St George High School, Manimala, to complete my high school. I had to walk 3 kilometres to the school, usually accompanied by classmates who lived in my neighbourhood. It was fun. I never participated in school events, except as a spectator. Nobody in school noticed that I existed. I was just another roll number in the school roll call. If I was absent, nobody enquired with my parents why I was absent. It was good to be anonymous. Nobody expects anything from you if you are anonymous.

This was where I tried to expand my activities. I joined the NCC. I didn't last long there. I tried my hand at sports. I joined the school football team where I was the goalkeeper. After an inter-school competition, in which I conceded three goals in fifteen minutes, I was sacked. I never played the game again. I went back to fooling around in the neighbourhood of my home, mostly with my siblings.

In the final year of my school, I got a pair of rubber chappals, a floater. I was the only one in the school with a rubber chappal. Everybody else was barefooted. I was so embarrassed. All the boys in the school had two shorts and three shirts for the school; the girls had one more. Nobody felt the need for anything more, not even the kids from well-off families. All the kids from the village went to the same school, the rich and the poor. There were no English-medium schools in the neighbourhood those days.

Finally, the moment of reckoning came: the class 10 board exams. I wrote the examination with a lot of trepidation, after a nightmarish experience with the headmaster, where he had strongly suggested that I should appear for the board exams the following year.

When the results came, the headmaster was shocked: I passed with 42 per cent. In most families in India, if their child scored 499 out of 500, the parents would howl at them: 'Where is that one mark gone?' In my house, my family was thrilled; I was on top of the world. We had a massive celebration.

One week after the results were out, a sobering thought began to settle in: what do I do with 42 per cent. I couldn't write or speak one sentence of English properly. Kerala had no jobs and to find employment one had to go out of the state; one had to know English and Hindi. My Malayalam was okay, but that would not have been of much help. I was a failure for the world.

The Take-Off

After the famous 42 per cent, I was never meant to be the neighbourhood hero. There were sarcastic remarks wherever I went. When I couldn't bear it any more, I decided to go fishing with my homemade fishing rod, just to escape the trauma. That fateful day, I was sitting on the trunk of a tree which was leaning towards the water, waiting for the fish to bite. I think I dozed off after a while and the fishing rod fell into the water. My only weapon to a meaningful world was gone! And then something happened. The thought of a world beyond my irrelevant life flashed before me. Suddenly two thoughts came to me. The first was 'I am not stupid. I have brains.' My second thought was 'I am not useless. I have talents.'

I don't think it was a divine revelation. It might have been be the delusions of a troubled mind, but I decided to listen to them.

This was the turning point in my life. I decided that it was not for my teachers, my parents or my neighbours to determine whether I was intelligent or if I had talents. I decided for myself that I was intelligent. I decided that I had talents.

I knew these would be empty words in the absence of anything on the table to prove my newfound belief. I was being presumptuous. I had to prove to myself that I was all these things which I began to imagine. I decided to work on myself.

So I enrolled in college. I had to catch up with those who were light-years ahead of me. I decided to teach myself the basics of being smart step by step. My first priority was to learn English. I started listening to the BBC news as often as I could. I wanted to speak English and speak it the way it should be spoken. I joined a phonetics course.

Oxford English Dictionary became my best friend. Every day I would study twenty-five pages of the dictionary. How does one study the dictionary? My method was simple: learn the meaning of the word and then make a sentence with it. A word makes sense only in a sentence. Then I used the phonetics experience to make sure that I pronounced these words properly. Once I had some vocabulary, I started reading English classics such as Charles Dickens, Jane Austin, Leo Tolstoy and Pablo Neruda. Wherever I found an interesting paragraph, I would try to transcribe it into my own words. Later, I would use them whenever the occasion arose. I devoured everything. I began to read Encyclopaedia Britannica. In three years, from the age of fifteen to eighteen, I read voraciously and managed to cover most of Encyclopaedia Britannica.

When I was confident of my ability to use the English language, a desire grew in my heart – I wanted to be an orator. I had already learnt many things unconventionally and for my oratorial ambition also I chose an unconventional method. I locked myself in my room and spoke to the wall for six months. It was not a secretive affair, as I was loud. Being loud is one of the things I carried through my life from this experiment because I knew that it was the best way of being heard. Later, this came in handy in politics. As an MP, most of the time I spoke without a mike as I was loud enough to be heard. The chairman of Rajya Sabha admonished me a few times for being so loud; I told him that it was in my DNA to be loud and I couldn't do anything about it. He had to suffer me because I guess I spoke sense.

Six months after my 'talking to the wall' experiment started, I ventured into taking part in a college-level debate competition with confidence. After all, I had put in so much effort. I had to be good. There were over 1000 students in the audience. A couple of minutes into my speech, some guys in the audience began to howl. It spread like an epidemic; I didn't stop. Then a few paper balls landed on the stage; I ignored it. The number of paper balls increased to a few hundred; I just raised my voice. A book was thrown at me, then a dozen books; they all missed the target. Then someone chucked a shoe at me. And it rained shoes all over the place. By the time I was finished, there were over a hundred shoes on the stage. Any sensible person would have run away from the stage long ago. I persisted till the end, shameless. There were enough shoes to start a shoe store. I was told by the organisers that I could not debate any more. I felt hopeless.

After a week, I decided that I was not giving up. I wanted to be a debater. This time, instead of the wall, I chose an open park as my laboratory. I requested some of my friends to help me out; they refused. They reminded me of the shoes on the stage. Six months later, I managed to enlist in a debate; I got no prize, but no shoes or books were thrown at me. I became a regular feature at most debate competitions. I didn't get a prize for a long time. Then I got a tiny prize, then a bigger one. After a long time, I won the best debater prize in the college, and I was on top of the world. I had finally arrived. Then I began to take part in inter-college and inter-university debate competitions. Initially I didn't do great; but I was not booted out. Eventually, in all-India inter-university debate competitions, I won the best debater prize two years in a row. A good part of my time in the university was spent travelling to take part in debate competitions across the country.

From the above narrative, if anybody thinks that I was a bookworm, they are hugely mistaken. I had all the fun. I was all over the place. I went to all the parties. I had shoulder-length hair because all of us tried to imitate the Beatles in some way or the other, as they were the craze of the decade.

I still listen to the Beatles a lot. I think they wrote and sang the best music ever. I loved Jim Reeves and Neil Diamond. They were the best soloists. Later, when Pink Floyd released their album *The Wall* in 1979, I got pretty crazy about them. I still listen to 'Brick in the Wall' at least once a week.

I was in the university drama team. I was also in the university choir. I never dared to be a solo performer; I was not good enough. But I felt comfortable being in the choir. When we performed Handel's 'Hallelujah Chorus', with over 200 participants, we were ecstatic. Our choirmaster, Brother McArthy, was a man of incredible talent. The university choir also had its benefits: the prettiest girls in the university were in the choir. Even though I was not the best-looking guy around the block, I was popular. At five feet eight, though I was not tall enough to be playing basketball, I played for the university team. I was fairly good. I went to every festival in town and to a lot of parties with a bunch of fun-loving friends. My friends were good in studies as well. I didn't do badly, in spite of being into a million things. There was one huge chasm between us though: they all loved math and I hated it.

I went to college with great apprehension, of being the dumbest kid in the world. I struggled very hard in college to find my roots. I was made fun of by kids from elite and not-so-elite schools. I suffered it all. It was tough and humiliating to begin with. But I had decided: I will make it. When I began to succeed, it was great fun. I came out of it with such incredible confidence, of being someone who could face the world, no matter what was in store.

I rocked. I decided that I could make a difference to the world in some way.

> Don't take no for an answer. You have the brain. You have the talents. You have to try hard enough.

2

Cracking the Impossible

IN THE FINAL SEMESTER of my postgraduate studies, I decided that I wanted to be in the Indian Administrative Service (IAS). I was deeply impressed by what district collectors and superintendents of police did.

For many Indian youth, cracking the civil service examination is the ultimate dream. The blockbuster movie *12th Fail* captures this desperation of the youth. Approximately 1.5 million candidates take a shot at the examinations, one of the toughest in the world, each year. Less than 200 people get into the Indian Administrative Service, about 40 get into the Indian Foreign Service (IFS) and about 100 into the Indian Police Service (IPS). All 23 civil services together induct about 900 candidates a year.

After my postgraduation, I enrolled at a small coaching centre in Pusa Road. Since I couldn't afford an independent accommodation, I decided to stay with my cousin Jose and his wife, Sonia, who graciously put me up.

I had just nine months to prepare for the examinations. I decided that I would attempt the examination just once, even though we had the right to appear for the examination thrice. Now candidates can appear six times and those in special categories can avail unlimited opportunities.

I had studied economics for both graduate and postgraduate studies. I was quite good at it, except for the mathematical portions. I found that economics was not a scoring subject in civil service examinations. I opted for three optionals I had never studied before: sociology, history and philosophy.

The first thing I did before I started studying was write in my diary: I am going to be in the Indian Administrative Service, and I am going to be one of the toppers. I know that it was presumptuous of me to write that. But after what I had done with my big makeover in college, I had the confidence and the temerity to write that.

Once I knew exactly what I wanted, I got down to planning how to do it. I made a timetable. Since I had nine months left for the examination, I decided that I would study for six months and the next three months I would revise. I decided that I would study only eight hours a day. I would spend the rest of the time with friends, listening to music, going on long walks, watching movies or just hanging out. For each day of the first six months, I made a detailed timetable, starting from the wake-up time to bedtime. Everything I did was in my timetable, including the time I would spend hanging out with friends. My timetable not only mentioned which subject I would study, say from 9 a.m. to 11 a.m., but also the exact chapters I would cover in the two hours. I filled in all the topics in my timetable; I started studying only after that. I would study a subject for a maximum of two hours. After that I would take a break for ten minutes before I started off with another subject. Generally, I would start studies at 9 a.m. and wind up by midnight, with a lot of things other than studies thrown in. I decided to stick by and large to some core textbooks. Only when I needed clarifications would I walk down to Lala Lajpat Rai library for reference. I had my way of writing notes: after I finished a chapter I would write a brief note, generally not more than three pages, in a notebook. All the main points would be numbered.

Within six months, I finished the first round of study of all the subjects as scheduled. I now had three months for revision. Again, the first thing I did was to draw up a timetable for three months so that I did not miss out on any topic. Still the maximum number of hours for study remained eight hours. This time, I changed my methodology for writing notes: my note for each chapter was limited to both sides of a library catalogue card. All the points were numbered, exactly in the logical order in which I would eventually write in the examination. After completing the note, I would go through the points a couple of times. Then I would close my eyes and try to recollect all the points the way it was numbered. If I missed a point, I would open my eyes, run through the note once more and then repeat the process of closing my eyes and recollecting the points, exactly in the serial order in which they were written. This helped me immensely because during the examination I could recollect the points exactly as they were in my note. I missed nothing.

When D-Day came, I was nervous. I am generally nervous before any examination. After the first paper I was distressed. I thought I didn't do well. The rest of the papers went well. When the examinations were over, I was hugely relieved. I had done the best I could. I was confident that I would qualify for the interview. As expected, I got through the written examinations, and I was called for the interview.

The wise people in the interview board generally consisted of former civil servants and subject experts. There were half a dozen interview boards, each headed by a member of the Union Public Service Commission (UPSC). Again, I got back to systematic preparations for the interview. I was confident that I would do well in the interview, since I was a national debater. There was no specific syllabus for the interview. They could ask anything under the sun. So the most critical thing to do was to be up to date with global and national current news. I would go to Lajpat Nagar library and read all the major newspapers and photocopy editorials and lead articles. I spent a lot of time at the Jawaharlal Nehru University (JNU) campus, meeting up with those who had qualified for the interview.

I made an attempt for a makeover in my appearance for the interview to look presentable. I still had the shoulder length hair from my university days. I got a decent haircut and tailored a navy-blue suit for the event. I got into a taxi and reached the UPSC office on Shahjahan Road well ahead of the interview.

I mustered all the courage and went into the interview when my turn came, with a huge smile on my face. After the formalities, they asked me about my views on prohibition – those were the days of Prime Minister Morarji Desai, prohibition and urine therapy. I spoke against prohibition even though I had never had a drink before. I believed that prohibition trampled upon the right to individual choice. The board didn't sound very happy. The next question was on India's foreign policy. Here, too, I strongly disagreed with the new thrust of India's foreign policy. Over the next forty-five minutes, I was grilled on everything except anything from the three optional subjects on which I had put so much of effort. I was vocal and logical, according to my perception, and I thought I sounded convincing, but since I spoke mostly against government policies I didn't see any nod of appreciation from the board. I thought I did well, expressing independent views. When the final result of the civil service examination was published in 1979, it was a shock to me to find that I got just 50 per cent in the interview. Being a national debater, I had expected to score really good in the interview. In spite of scoring badly, I still ended up being one of the toppers of the IAS examination, as I had scored exceptionally well in the written examinations, including the first paper, which I thought I had done badly.

In my batch, there were only 120 persons selected to the IAS. All services put together, there were around 400 of us.

Even though I could have chosen the IFS, as one of the toppers, I chose the IAS, because I was interested in working only in India. I wanted to make India better.

Mine was a good lesson on how not to face an interview. Mine was a problem of over confidence. I keep advising civil service aspirants that they should never do what I did. There were a million better ways of saying the same things, even the most unconventional views, which don't put off the board and establishment. You have to be diplomatic and clever. I was not.

Finally, I was one of God's chosen ones (that is how the civil service considers itself to be. It is rubbish.). I was going to be a district collector.

> A prerequisite for success is a big dream. Plan in detail how to get there. Follow the plan. Put your heart and soul into it.

3

Life at the IAS Academy

My village gave me a massive reception when I went home after getting into the IAS. I was the first one to get into the IAS from my village. My picture was published prominently in all Malayalam newspapers. All the schools that I had studied in, nearby churches, temples and mosques gave me a rousing reception. I was the new hero in the village.

One had to prepare carefully to join the Lal Bahadur Shastri National Academy of Administration (LBSNAA), Mussoorie, up in the hills at 2000 metres above sea level. It was about ten hours away from Delhi in those days. A blue blazer and a bandh gala (a button-up jacket covering one's neck) were mandatory. I bought a woollen blue blazer at Delhi from Mohanlal Sons' for ₹300. It is now almost half-a-century old, and I still use it extensively. It is still in great shape.

I went to the academy, got into grey trousers, a blue blazer and a tie. I became a 'probationer'. I hated that word. It was as if one was an under trial. They don't call them 'probationers' any more at LBSNNA. They are called 'trainee officers'.

Even though I had fairly long hair, I tried to look decent. But I was unsure whether I would ever be an ideal probationer and live up to the expectations of my bosses at the academy. I came to the IAS academy filled with idealism. I believed that anybody from the civil services could do miracles. After spending forty-five years in the IAS, social work and politics, I retain my belief. I am an eternal optimist. I hate people making excuses for non-performance. For me, performance was not about writing beautiful notes on files; it was about bringing happiness on the face of people in every situation, through actual delivery on the ground, not just on social media.

At heart, I was always a rebel, sometimes with a cause and sometimes without. I never accepted anything without questioning, including the holy book of All India Service Rules, which I refused to read till I quit the IAS twenty-seven years later.

For the foundation course, there were about 400 of us; a foundation course at the academy lasted for three months. All the probationers who got into service in that particular year were there. We developed a great sense of camaraderie, which has lasted even post-retirement. After the foundation course, IAS officers continued with Phase 1 of the professional course at the academy, while those belonging to other services went to their respective academies. After Phase 1 of professional course, we had district training for almost a year in the state to which we were allotted. We returned to the academy after that to complete three months of Phase 2 of professional training.

We were woken up early at 5 a.m. for the physical training (PT). Imagine getting up so early in a hill station, where the temperatures dip quite low. I hated PT. Instead of PT, I chose to jog to Company Bagh and back with my friend Sanjay Dasgupta, who was a rebel against all things establishment. I got sixteen notices for skipping PT. But the idea stuck with me that physical fitness was critical for doing a good job and leading a meaningful life. I have kept up with jogging for the past forty-five years. When I go the academy once in a while as a guest speaker, I always join the PT.

We spent a lot of time at a cafe everyone called Hari's cafe. Hari also sold books. I bought a lot of books, mostly existentialist literature. I loved Kafka and Sartre. Hari was a great friend of generations of probationers. Hari's is where most of the academy romances took root.

Our Mussoorie days were fun. We hung around the front lawn most of the time, with lovely pine trees towering over us. Most of us didn't take the lectures seriously, as most of them were boring and irrelevant. Even the lectures by our joint director about how he shot down eighteen civilians in eighteen minutes as a district magistrate in a northeastern state, which we young probationers mistook for acts of heroism, sounds sadistic now when we look back after dealing with real-life events. We often found refuge at the residence of our deputy director N.C. Saxena and his most affable wife, Naomi, whose house was always open to probationers. But there were a few probationers, whom we called KTPs (keen-type probationers), who devoured every word, as they were all aspirants for the Director's Gold Medal.

Everybody who comes to the academy is brilliant. It has to be so due to the selection process that weeds out candidates from 1.5 million to a few hundred. There is only one thing which ensures whether they will do any good to the nation: attitude. I strongly believed that the academy should be a place where we should imbibe a strong sense of integrity and commitment to the nation and the job. Mussoorie should be the place which reinforces one's backbone.

Today, when you go to the Mussoorie academy, you don't see a soul on the lawn; you don't see anybody hanging around with friends. Regimentation at LBSNNA has become something like a military academy. Students are deeply involved with academics and projects from morning to late at night. I am told that the academy now offers diploma courses in association with global institutions as an optional subject, after regular classes. They have no time to socialise or talk about the problems plaguing humanity at large. There is little talk about attitude.

If the objective of the training at Mussoorie was to create specialists, why recruit generalists at all? They should just do campus recruitment for each category of specialisation. If you wanted people who specialise in engineering, IITs would be a good place.

I had organised many debates and discussions as secretary of the Fine Arts Club. We had a lot of musical talent around, with Tapan Senapati, BKD and Baggi playing the guitar. Seini sang better than any lead vocalists of the time. Ramendra was deeply into Indian classical music. Aditi set the dance floor on fire wherever she went. Once Aditi and I partnered to win the Mussoorie open contest. We won only because Aditi moves the planet when she is on the floor. Later, in her job, Aditi was one of the finest officers in the civil service. Kush won every sports event.

Since Sanjay and I were broke all the time, Sanjay's fiancé, Shangun, who was teaching at a school in Mussoorie, fed us all the time. Sanjay, who was a history graduate, pioneered computerisation of rural information as a sub collector. He went on to become the first Information Technology Secretary of Karnataka. He was exceptional in everything he did. Unfortunately, he passed away early in life. I miss him a lot.

I think that the best thing our gang did was outside the academy. We started a campaign to stop unbridled exploitation of Mussoorie by the mining companies. Mussoorie hills have large deposits of limestone, an essential component of cement. We found that the entire Mussoorie range was being hugely over exploited. Mussoorie was dying. My gang decided that it had to be stopped. We made a representation to the district collector at Dehradun and to the chief minister to stop the mining of Mussoorie hills. But there was no response. We came to the conclusion that paperwork would not produce any result. We decided to change strategy. On a Sunday, my gang trekked down

33 kilometres to the collector's residence at Dehradun. We gave him a memorandum to stop the mining. He said that mining was essential for the economy. We told him that economic development was fine, but we would not allow destruction of our hills. But the collector wouldn't relent. We threatened to sit in dharna in front of his residence on the main road. When he didn't yield, we made good on our threat. A lot of curious onlookers gathered around. When they learnt of the cause and that we were IAS probationers, they joined us in solidarity. Within three hours, the collector issued orders under Section 133 of Criminal Procedure Code, banning mining in Mussoorie hills.

I look back at the IAS Academy with nostalgia. The best part of the training period was the village visit. We were sent in groups of twenty-five each to the remotest villages in the country. My group spent two weeks in Patalkot, in Chhindwara district of Madhya Pradesh. Patalkot was one of the most backward villages in the country. We had to walk for hours to reach the village. We were lucky that there was a two-room primary school in the village which had benches and desks on which we could sleep. However, there were no toilets. We were out with the villagers the whole day and ate the local food. The village visit left an indelible mark in our hearts. We knew what we would do going forward.

One of the most exciting events during academy training was the trek. We were again sent in groups of twenty-five each on treks in the Himalayas for fifteen days. We could choose treks of varying toughness. Many chose tough treks, going up to 18,000 feet. My group was dropped at Rudraprayag, located at an altitude of 2,936 feet. We trekked for the next fifteen days to Kedarnath, Badrinath, Valley of Flowers and Hemkund. There were no proper roads those days. We slept in one room in forest guard quarters on the way, men and women. We were provided with half the number of blankets and pillows, because that is all they had, and we shared them. Valley of Flowers was absolutely spectacular. We had to mandatorily bathe in the lake at Gurdwara Hemkund Sahib, located at an elevation of 15,000 feet. The lake was partly frozen. I still feel a chill going through my bones thinking about it. But it was an incredible experience.

Another exciting event of the academy was the military attachment. My group was attached to 4th Para in Gangtok, which was deployed at Nathu La, a major theatre of confrontation with China in 1967. It was also a major trade centre between India and China. All of us were dumped at the back of a military truck and the road to Nathu La was tough. We could see the Chinese soldiers face to face. A visit to Baba Harbhajan Singh Memorial, built in memory of Harbhajan Singh, a sepoy who lost his life in the 1962 India–China war, took us back to the days of the 1962 war and the bravery of our men. Evenings were fun with Colonel Dutt, the commanding officer, and Major Michelangelo, who was injured seriously in the 1971 India–Pakistan war, making great efforts to entertain us in the bar. Lights went off in the bar pretty late during our attachment.

After I became the tourism minister of India in 2017, I went back to Nathu La with my wife. The road to Nathu La was now black topped. India has built an incredible infrastructure at Nathu La. Nobody is going to walk over India.

I don't think that I was an ideal probationer by any means. I never skipped a class. I asked plenty of questions. Yet my bosses at the academy, Ramki and Muthuswamy, didn't approve of me. I don't blame them. I was never the conventional definition of a probationer. I was not a conventional IAS officer either. I did things my way. But I was clear about what I wanted from my job: a smile on the faces of our citizens. That's a tough job. If you don't deliver day after day what the citizen wants, the smile disappears. People say that I have been phenomenally successful (I have more than twenty-five editorials, not just lead articles, in leading newspapers on me. I have ten cartons of clippings on my work). I was in *Time* magazine's list of 100 young global leaders. Yet I have a billion reasons to be modest about, because I never felt that I was bigger than the lowliest citizen. Anyway, what I did was just a drop in the ocean; but it was definitely a drop.

I loved the academy.

> It is not intelligence that matters, it is attitude.

4

Mangaladevi: Where a God Was Threatened

M.G. RAMACHANDRAN, POPULARLY KNOWN as MGR, was the chief minister of Tamil Nadu from 1977 to 1987. Considered one of the most popular stars of Tamil cinema, he was a demigod for the people of Tamil Nadu. He still is. Transitioning from a big-time movie star to politics was a smooth affair for him. He was at the height of his power when I threatened to arrest him.

Here is the story:

In 1981 July, I finished my training at the IAS Academy and took over as the sub collector of Devikolam, just 7 kilometres from Munnar, a hill station perched at 3000 feet above sea level. Munnar is best known for its tea plantations. Way back in 1877, John Munro, a British, received 1,36,600 acres of forest land on lease from the King of Poonjar and raised some of the best tea plantations in the world. The tea produced was exported to Great Britain. They even built a rail system to transport tea from Munnar to Hilltop, near Mattupetty, from where it was sent down to the valley through ropeways. The rail got washed away in the 1940 floods.

It was barely a year into my first assignment as the sub collector when things heated up on the Kerala–Tamil Nadu border, at Thekkady, in my jurisdiction. Thekkady is where the Mullaperiyar dam is located. The Periyar Wildlife

Sanctuary is also here. The wildlife sanctuary has been one of the most successful Project Tiger programmes.

About 10 kilometres from Thekkady is located the Mangaladevi temple.[1] It is right on top of the hill where the boundary of Kerala and Tamil Nadu is demarcated. It is a 1000-year-old ancient temple. It has a fascinating story: Kannagi, the devoted wife of Kovalan, took revenge against those who killed her husband in a false cheating case. She burnt down the entire Madurai city and reached the Suruli hills. From here she ascended into heaven along with her husband in a Pushpaka Viman. Inspired by this legend, the Tamilakam king Cheran Chenguttuvan built the Mangaladevi temple in her honour and deified her. The renowned Tamil poet Ilango Adigal wrote the epic *Silappathikaram* based on this story.

Mangaladevi temple is open to devotees only during the time of Chitra Pournami. Both Tamilians and Keralites used to offer worship here. They co-existed peacefully for decades. In 1982, when MGR was the chief minister, he announced that the temple was located in Tamil Nadu and that he was coming to take possession of the temple and offer prayers.[2]

I collected the relevant survey records and went to the site with the concerned Kerala government officials. It was clear from the maps that the temple was located in Kerala. I promptly sent a letter. I said that the chief minister was most welcome to come and offer prayers at the temple and that he would be received with honour and protocol.

Prompt came the reply, reiterating the chief minister's stand that the temple belongs to Tamil Nadu and that the chief minister would visit the temple in about ten days' time. They built a helipad near the temple in Tamil Nadu territory, as there was no road access to the temple from the Tamil Nadu side. Preparations were made on a war footing for the chief minister's 'conquest' of Mangaladevi.

Keralites were furious at the threat of invasion by Tamil Nadu. It was as if Tamil Nadu was going to take over Kerala. Media in both the states picked it up as a top story.

I camped in Thekkady. Just two days before the scheduled arrival of the chief minister, I issued an order under section 144 of Criminal Procedure Code, banning the chief minister from coming to Mangaladevi as it would cause serious law and order problem. There was shock and anger in Tamil Nadu. Some organisations in Tamil Nadu declared a price of ₹50,000 on my head. I didn't know that my head was so valuable. In 1982, ₹50,000 was a large amount. My basic pay as sub collector was only ₹740. Ever since I have learnt to live life dangerously.

I moved closer to the theatre of action. I pitched a tent next to the temple. We also put up tents for police, forest and revenue officials. I had a police force with me. So did the other side. The district collector panicked and sent the additional district magistrate to take charge of the situation. I told him that this was my jurisdiction and that he had nothing to do with this. He wouldn't leave. I had to threaten to use my magisterial powers to throw him out.

On D-Day, I was ready to arrest the chief minister of Tamil Nadu. He was to land at 11 a.m. There was considerable tension all over. People from both states gathered on both sides of the hill and shouted slogans. It looked like tribal warfare. I waited with bated breath for the sound of the chopper. The countdown started at 10.50 a.m. Just ten minutes to go. 9 … 8 … 7 … 6 … 5 … 4 … 3 … 2 … 1 … 0. There was no chopper in sight. It was another two hours before we got to know from the radio that MGR had called off his invasion. There were celebrations on the Kerala side. The scene on the other side looked distressing. It took a long time for them to come to terms with the news. They could not believe that their demigod had backed out under threat. Nobody had expected the great MGR to back out on the threat of a twenty-eight-year-old sub collector who was barely a year into his first job. I was quite sure that he would back out, for the simple reason that he would never be able to live with the thought of a petty official arresting him. He would never be able to live with it if the crazy sub collector went ahead with his threat.

It has been over forty years now. They have not withdrawn the price on my head. Hopefully my head is worth much less, now that I hit seventy. But even now, when I travel in Tamil Nadu, I don't reveal my name. Some people can be fanatics when it comes to their gods.

Many pilgrims from Tamil Nadu come to the temple for worship during the season every year and it is well organised by the Kerala Forest Department.

The incident, right at the beginning of my long career in the IAS, taught me a lot of things, which became the foundation for the rest of my career. I learnt to take independent decisions. I learnt that irrespective of the risk involved one has to do one's duty. I decided that I will never be cowed down by threats, even from the most powerful people.

What I did was not taught in the IAS Academy.

Be cool; don't get frazzled when big forces are threatening you.

5

The Old Man and a Small Fish

There is a well-known story about a young boy who was visiting a beach one summer when he saw thousands of small fish being washed ashore. He noticed an old man pick up the stranded fish, one by one, and throw them back into the ocean.

Walking up to the old man he said, 'Hello, old man. I have been watching you. You must be a lunatic. There are thousands of fish being washed ashore and most of them die. You are rescuing just a few. Don't you think it is a waste of time? Why don't you just go to one of the shacks by the beach, have a beer and relax?'

The man didn't say anything. He took a few steps, bent down and picked up a fish and threw it into the water and the fish swam off. Then he told the youngster, 'I made a difference in the life of that fish.' He then picked up another fish, which was desperately trying to catch its breath, and threw it into the sea. Then another one.

The young boy was lost for words. He joined the man for the next hour. Together they threw dozens of fish back into the water. Before he left, the boy said to the old man, 'Today has been my biggest learning experience. I now know that I cannot save everybody on the planet, but I can save a few. That will also make my life meaningful.'

For most of us, who think we are completely helpless in the face of the enormous problems of the planet, this story can start a new chapter in our lives.

One such person who was deeply inspired by this story is Amal Saji from Karuvatta in Alappuzha district of Kerala. When he was in class 10, he, along with a bunch of close friends in school, set up the Snehasparsham movement in their village in 2018. 'Snehasparsham' means 'a touch of love'. The first thing they did was to establish the Snehasparsham library. They built a thatched shed in the panchayat land, with the approval of the panchayat committee. The team got a few thousand books through door-to-door collection. Most of them were children's books. They managed to get all the leading newspapers and magazines sponsored by families. They lobbied with parents to send their children to the library after school hours. And so the library became a hub of activities, where children read books, discussed news, played games, learnt to debate and cleaned the neighbourhood. Everything was managed by the children.

Then they decided that they could help the villagers receive benefits under government schemes. They called the project 'samaswasa'. They conducted classes for villagers to familiarise them with government schemes. They helped them to fill up the relevant application forms and follow up with government offices for necessary approvals. After one year of the library's launch, Amal stepped down from the position of president and established a permanent child administration through elections. Henceforth, the positions of library president, secretary and all other posts were to be filled by children, elected by the members.

This initiative had a significant impact. Snehasparsham Library is now renowned as Kerala's first library managed by children and acknowledged by the Kerala State Child Rights Commission. They started providing assistance to the unemployed to find jobs in 2021. In collaboration with corporate bodies, they organised recruitment camps. In 2022, Amal and his friends conducted workshops in 147 schools on responsible parenting and child protection, with the help of experts. They organised fifty-five 'child safety campaigns', throughout Alappuzha district, benefiting 5000 children. They launched a 'Internet Safety for Children' campaign throughout the district.

Snehasparsham extended its activities to six districts of Kerala. All the activities are coordinated by school and college-going kids.

The library not only sparked a knowledge revolution within the village but also significantly uplifted the lives of many children. One such individual is Mubeena, a tenth-grade student who was hesitant to participate in school programmes as she was shy. Without any clear future goals, she initially considered pursuing a paramedical course. However, after becoming a member of the library, she was encouraged to run in the library's administrative elections and won the position of vice president. This role required her to interact with thousands of people and she organised over twenty programmes, enhancing her speaking, leadership and organisational skills. These experiences boosted her confidence and self-determination. Mubeena is now pursuing an LLB from Kerala University and is a leading young social worker in Karuvatta.

Another notable example is Thomas, a seventh-grade student with attention-deficit hyperactive disorder (ADHD). His parents were exasperated by his constant noise and hyperactivity at home, and he showed no interest in studies. However, after joining the library, he was appointed as the leader of the reading club and assigned with various tasks. The transformation was remarkable. Thomas excelled in storytelling and won a prize for creating crafts from waste materials during a Gandhi Jayanti celebration. He began caring for other members and taking on leadership roles. Within three months, Thomas became the library's best performer. He is now an excellent storyteller and has taken up drawing. He has become focused on his studies, securing top rank in the entrance exam for admission to a technical school.

Amal and his friends decided to go beyond Kerala and set up Gandhi Darshan Library in Champaran in Bihar. The focus of the Champaran library is literacy. They are also deeply involved in building leadership among children in the village, so that they can do their bit in improving the living conditions in the village. School enrolment has improved considerably after establishment of the library in Shuklahi village. The library has earned lot of goodwill in the community.

Amal has moved to Haryana recently. He is based at Pundri in Kaithal district. He works with the local MLA, to whom he has been able to sell the idea of youth responsibility and community involvement.

Amal has not yet decided what he wants to with his life. In my last meeting with him, I tried to persuade him to get into the civil service. I don't know whether I managed to convince him. He is also interested in politics. He will make a difference wherever he is.

Amal's life changed dramatically with the story of the tiny fish on a beach. He has touched the lives of thousands of 'fish' in a short time, and his life has just begun.

> You can't save the whole world. But you can, through small acts, make a big difference in the lives of some people.

6

Alchemy of a Dreamer

P. Vijayan's is a more exciting story than the protagonist of the phenomenally successful movie *12th Fail*, a story about the tribulations and the ecstasy of a rural youth, who got into the Indian Police Service. Vijayan was appointed the additional director general (ADG) of police in Kerala in 2024. He belongs to the 1999 batch of the Indian Police Service.

As a young boy, Vijayan stood ankle-deep in mud in paddy fields along with his parents, trying to eke out a living. He did many things while in school, be it selling peanuts for a profit of just ₹1 or collecting mussels from the sea and selling it to neighbours. Naturally, studies suffered. As expected, he failed to clear the class 10 board examination and dropped out of school.

By then, he was old enough to bear bigger loads on his shoulders and he started working as a construction worker. He was earning money to support his family. After a while, he felt that something was missing: the joy of learning from books. So, he joined night classes after working hours. He passed school. But still he had to work as a construction worker to survive. He went on to complete the pre-degree course, again as a part-time private student. He was now sure that to make it anywhere in life he had to go to college as a full-time student. Subsequently, he joined a full-time graduate course in economics at Zamorin's Guruvayurappan College, Kozhikode.

But being a member of a family with seven children, Vijayan could not afford to go for higher studies without finding provision to meet the expenses – not only for his studies but also for his family. So he took a loan and started a soap manufacturing unit at home. He also supported his elder brother's business that filled up mattresses with cotton. None of his entrepreneurial ventures flourished for long, but he completed graduation. He enrolled for postgraduation in economics at Government Arts and Science College, Kozhikode, and then did a Bachelor of Education course in the hope that he would be able to become a schoolteacher. He generated enough income to meet his requirements by taking tuition classes for school students.

But then the civil service bug got to him and he plunged into full-time preparations for the civil service examinations, after some friends agreed to lend him enough money to pursue his dreams. He cleared the UPSC examinations in the first attempt itself and was chosen for Central Secretariat Services, whose personnel manage the middle-level administrative positions in the Central Secretariat. Even though that was way beyond what the young boy, standing ankle-deep in mud once, could cherish even in his wildest dreams, Vijayan wanted more. At the next attempt, he got into the Railway Protection Force. At the third attempt, in 1999, he got into the prestigious Indian Police Service and was allotted Kerala cadre.

Life also introduced him to Dr M. Beena, a brilliant young doctor with postgraduation in gynaecology, who went on to clear the IAS examination. They got married.

Vijayan realised that he had managed to turn around his life from the brink of losing it all. He could vouch for the amazing possibilities that education could offer. The eye-opener came when he encountered an entire generation lost to the world of narcotics and crime, during his posting as the city police commissioner of his home district, Kozhikode. That was the trigger that Vijayan needed. He went on to design a bouquet of programmes addressing various issues haunting young people and children – 'Student Police Cadets (SPC)' for crafting responsible citizenry, 'Our Responsibility to Children' to address juvenile delinquency, 'Project Hope' to support slow learners and dropouts, and 'Capability Exploration and Enhancement Programme (CEEP)' to identify and encourage gifted children in their special skills. He designed child-friendly police stations to address issues of children in contact and conflict with law.

His projects, such as the SPC programme, caught the attention of not just the country, but counterparts across the globe. The project is now implemented in around 13,000 schools across India and enquiries for the same have come from many countries. The conviction in the power of dreams got translated into a wonderful model that the whole world wants to emulate.

Vijayan's journey was noticed by the world as he was conferred with the Indian President's Police Medal for Meritorious Service in 2015, Union Home Minister's Utkrisht Seva Medal in 2021, Chief Minister's Award for Public Policy Innovation in 2014 and 2017, Rotary Lifetime Achievement Award, Champion of the Children Award instituted by the Delhi Commission for Protection of Child Rights, Government of Delhi and FICCI Award for 'Best SMART Policing Initiative'. He was chosen as the winner of the CNN-IBN Indian of the Year (Popular Choice) Award in 2014.

The remarkable journey that P. Vijayan made, from a child labourer to one of the most decorated police officers in the world, who could make significant social interventions, especially among youth and children, is testimony to the fact that once you have mastered the alchemy of dreams, what remains is the will to pursue it without losing focus.

His outstanding work as a police officer, and his social engagements has been the source for many books.

He is still young and you will hear plenty about him in the future.

> You can dream big, irrespective of your family background.

7

Golden Sheetal

TEENAGED ARMLESS ARCHER Sheetal Devi won three medals – two gold and a silver – in archery in Asia Para Games, held at Hangzhou in October 2023. She became the first woman to win two golds medals in a single edition. She won the individual compound archery gold. Initially she was lagging, but then she shot 10s in the last six shots. She also won the compound mixed team gold in partnership with Rakesh Kumar and silver in the women's doubles, partnering Sarita. She won the bronze medal at the 2024 Paralympics in the mixed team compound event. She is only sixteen and has an incredible life ahead of her.

Sheetal was born armless at birth, in the remote Loi Dhar village in Kishtwar, Jammu and Kashmir, in a poor family. Her father works as an agriculture labourer in the fields, and her mother tends to half a dozen family goats. Sheetal suffers from Phocomelia, a disease where organs remain underdeveloped. Her parents were deeply distressed at her birth, and understandably so. But they were happy to have a baby girl. Neighbours ridiculed the family. They said it was karma, meaning that it was retribution for the wrongs done in some other birth. But her parents loved her deeply and raised her with great dignity and had faith that she would make it on her own someday.

Growing up was tough for little Sheetal. Very few wanted to be friends with an armless kid because she couldn't play with them. Her world was her inner self and a close-knit family. Like all kids, she wanted friends to share her world. It was tough. But a few stuck to her.

At fourteen, she had no clue about archery. Her journey began in 2021, when she participated at an archery competition, organised by the Indian Army, in Kishtwar. The organisers were impressed by her enthusiasm. The army adopted her. They put her in touch with the Major Akshay Girish Memorial Trust in Bangalore, where they tried to fit her with an artificial arm. But the arm didn't fit her. Her world almost collapsed. But she didn't give up. She enrolled at Sri Mata Vaishno Devi Board Academy. A special bow was prepared for her; she could lift it with her feet. She could pull the arrow from her shoulder, using her chin and teeth to shoot. She was coached by Abhilasha Chaudhary and Kuldeep Vedwan. After a few months, she started practising with general category archers. She was hugely inspired by Matt Stutzman, who won silver in archery at the 2012 Paralympics. Matt doesn't have hands either.

After winning three medals, her reaction was: 'Initially, I could not even lift the bow properly. But after practicing for a couple of months, it became easier. My parents always had faith in me. My friends in the village also supported me. The only thing I didn't like was the look on people's face when they realised that I didn't have arms. These medals prove that I am special. These medals are not just mine, but of the whole country.'[1] At sixteen, she is the most celebrated archer in the country. India has never been prouder.

The prime minister of India Narendra Modi tweeted: 'Proud of Sheetal Devi on her extraordinary Gold Medal in Archery Women's Individual Compound open event at the Asian Para Games. This achievement is a testament to her grit and determination.'[2]

Global innovative industrialist Anand Mahendra, Chairman of the Mahendra group, which is one of the biggest manufacturers of SUVs and tractors in the country, tweeted: 'I will never, EVER complain about petty problems in my life. Sheetal Devi, you are a teacher to us all. Please pick any car from our range and we will award it to you and customise it for your use.'[3]

Prachi Yadav, who is paralysed from the waist down, won the gold in the 500 metres KL2 event in canoeing. She also won a silver. She was the first Indian to win a para canoe gold in Asian Para Games. Her husband, Manish Kaurav, who had battled locomotive disorder from birth, won a bronze in the men's canoe KL3 event. 'Winning a medal for the country is a special feeling, but this is something special for both of us. We won't forget this day,' they said.[4] Manish said of his wife: 'She inspires me. I always think that if she can achieve success, I too can.'[5]

This Paralympics was also historic for India, winning seven medals in blind chess.

India won 111 medals at the 2023 Para Asian Games at Hangzhou. This was the highest medal tally for India at any major multisport event, surpassing the Asian Games tally of 107, held in the same city. Government support to the game, through the Khelo India initiative and the Target Olympic Podium Scheme (TOPS), has produced remarkable results.

There are soul-moving stories of other para-athletes who have fought their disabilities to conquer the world. Let me mention three of them:

Tanni Grey, on a wheelchair, won sixteen medals (eleven golds, four silvers and a bronze). She became a television commentator for BBC. In 2010, she was made a life peer of the House of Lords. She is now a baroness.

Ellie Simmonds, classified as Anchodroplasia dwarf at only 1.23 metres tall, won two gold medals in swimming at 2008 Beijing Summer Paralympics for the United Kingdom at the age of thirteen in 100 metres and 400 metres races. Again, in the London Paralympics, she won 400 metres freestyle gold, 200 metres medley gold, 100 metres silver and 50 metres bronze. In total, she won five Paralympics gold, eight world championship gold, six world championship and seven European championship gold. Ellie was appointed a Member of the Order of the British Empire at fourteen years old, the youngest ever.

Trischa Zorn is a blind American Paralympics swimmer. She is the most successful athlete in the history of Paralympics, having won fifty-five medals (forty-one gold, nine silver and five bronze).

These amazing people show that we can achieve whatever we want, in spite of all the handicaps. None of us are born perfect. We have got to make best use of whatever we have.

> It takes persistence and perseverance to be a winner.

8

The Voice of the Oppressed

REGI GEORGE AND Lalitha Regi are an unusual doctor couple.

Regi comes from a land-owning Syrian Christian family in Central Kerala, while Lalitha comes from the royal family that once ruled Cochin. After their schooling, they both ended up as classmates in the Government TD Medical College in Alappuzha. During the third year they became part of the college union and this is when they came to know each other closely. They realised that they had the common dream of working with the underprivileged after their studies, and with this shared dream, they decided to get married. They then went on to finish their postgraduation – Regi in Anaesthesia at Manipal and Lalitha in Gynaecology from Trivandrum.

After their studies, they started working at Kasturba Hospital in Gandhigram, Dindigul, Tamil Nadu, in 1987. At that time, they were strictly clinical doctors, but during their five years there, they realised that clinical medicine was not the way that could bring health to a community. They were also attracted to the Gandhian idea of Gram Swaraj: self-reliance in everything. They wondered, 'Can self-reliance be applied to health also? Can communities be trained to look after their health, however remote or unschooled they were?'

Medical colleges teach nothing about the larger aspects of health – or the problems of the rural areas. To discover this, Regi did a *Bharat Yatra* – with a fellowship to support his travel, he backpacked through most of India – to see, to feel and to learn. During his early travel, he happened to be in Hemalkasa, where Dr Prakash and his wife Dr Manda worked with tribals in Maharashtra. Since both of them were on leave, he was requested to be the stand in doctor – where he came in close proximity to the health problems of the tribals, their helplessness and their inaccessibility to proper healthcare. From then on, he travelled only to tribal areas and spent a lot of time staying with the tribals.

After a year's travel, the couple decided to look for a place to work, possibly in a backward tribal area and they zeroed in on the Sittilingi Valley in Dharmapuri, Tamil Nadu.

Sittilingi Valley is surrounded by the Kalrayan and Sitheri Hills, a closed verdant hollow, crisscrossed by fast running jungle streams. The valley has 25 hamlets of about 15,000 people, 95 per cent of whom are from the Malavasi (hill dweller) tribe – the rest being made up of Lambadis and Dalits. The couple fell in love with the place and decided to move in and make it their 'karma bhoomi' in 1993. But it was not without its problems. The nearest town was 50 kilometres away. Health statistics were depressing: the IMR (infant mortality rate) was 147/1000, which meant that almost one child in five died before it reached the first birthday. Many mothers died during childbirth.

The couple registered their organisation as a public charitable trust along with some friends in 1992 and called it the 'Tribal Health Initiative'. As their tagline, they chose 'redefining health'.

They sat down with the local tribal folk and discussed the opening of a medical facility. Since they had no money, a vacant government wasteland of one acre was selected and the tribals brought in wood, thatch and helped them make a hut, which served as the hospital. Since there was no place to stay, the doctor couple and their three-year-old son stayed in a rented house, about 10 kilometres away in the nearest non-tribal village. They had a small bike on which they commuted to the 'Hut Hospital' and started to look at patients. Luck came in the first year itself, when a donor agency appreciated their work and donated funds to build a ten-bedded hospital, a training centre and a residential quarter for themselves. It was built by 1997 and with the coming up of a proper operation theatre, labour room and wards, much more advanced care could be given than what the 'Hut Hospital' delivered.

Regi and Lalitha did not forget that the purpose of their work was to find a way to help communities look after themselves. So they went out into the villages to search for girls who had gone to school. Since the valley had schools that only offered classes up to class 8, all they could find were girls educated till class 8, but Regi was willing to hire them. With great difficulty they were able to convince some parents to send their girls and thus the Health Worker Training Programme started. It was a one-year residential training. They found that the girls were smart and willing to learn, and within a year they learnt to diagnose and treat most common illness.

However, though the health workers would work in the newly built hospital, the community work had still not started in earnest. The doctors went to each village and sat down with the community and asked them to select one middle-aged lady, whom they could train. These candidates were called 'Health Auxiliaries', and they had never gone to school. They were trained for two days every fortnight for the next one and a half years. At the end of this, they knew the basics of sanitation and hygiene. They also learnt about nutrition, mother and child care and, most of all, developed communication skills on how to impart their knowledge to the community. They formed the cornerstone of the health intervention; with the fieldwork which was initiated by the hospital, infant mortality was brought down to 15/1000 and no mothers have died during childbirth for the past fifteen years – a creditable achievement, considering the geography they were working in.

By 2004, ten years of work had been completed and they now thought of branching out to start looking at the determinants of health. They did a *padayatra* to all the twenty-five villages, sitting down with the community and talking of their problems and how they, as a community, could try to solve them. Many suggestions came, but what the people needed most was help with farming, the only trade they knew. As an organisation believing in Gandhian values, it was not possible to support pesticide-dependent farming, but the farmers did not have faith in organic farming. Talks and meetings went on for two years before the first four farmers decided to try it out – and noticed that they actually made a profit from it. Next year, more joined and in the next few years, they had enough farmers to start their own Sittilingi Organic Farmers Association (SOFA) – which now has 700 organic certified farmers and their own production centre and is a training centre for many farmers in south India. With a turnover of more than 1.5 crore, it is one of the largest small farmer collectives in the country.

Next, they set up self-help groups for women, mainly to have a platform where the group borrows money to start small activities which can bring in money. They also have monthly savings, which they use for their house expenses, but the borrowed money is to be used to generate income. They were able to start with small soft loans from credible agencies, including NABARD and from friends, and started off with buying cattle. They also started their own cattle insurance. In a few years, the capital multiplied, and now they no longer need to borrow from outside – the 480 women, organised into 40 groups, have a capital of ₹1.6 crore, used for rotating loans and for building up their micro economy.

Next, Lalitha revived the Lambadi hand embroidery art, with just two elderly women, who had learnt the work from their grandmothers; she started teaching the younger generation about their cultural heritage. Slowly, the group started getting bigger and now there are sixty artisans and ten tailors, who have organised themselves into a society called *Porgai* – which means pride in their dialect. In 2023, they had a sale of ₹80 lakh, of which ₹20 lakh went back to the women of these two small villages.

By 2018, Sittilingi had faced a drought for three years, and wells no longer yielded water. Agriculture became a nightmare and many had to migrate to cities in search of livelihoods. So the couple started a watershed programme with the villagers through *shramdan* – mainly desilting the check dams, making farm ponds and spring stops. The industry too chipped in with CSR funds. Next year rains came and much of the water was stopped from flowing out of the valley and the wells were recharged. This brought great happiness to the farmers, but the doctors realised that for real infrastructure development they needed government funds and this can only be done through the panchayat.

A grassroots campaign was started for increasing awareness about the Gram Sabha, and people were actively mobilised to attend them and ask questions about fund utilisation. When the Panchayat elections were announced in 2019, the Farmers Association decided to put forward their own candidates, with no political affiliation. They won with a considerable majority, reaffirming the belief that ordinary people will always vote for an uncorrupted system. The present sarpanch is one of the senior nurses in the hospital. Having the panchayat in peoples' hands completely revolutionised the administrative system. A strict no corruption principle is followed, and now everyone has access to water, electricity and roads. Health took a great leap forward with this and the doctors suddenly realised that this is what Gram Swaraj means – people taking control of their lives.

Through Rural Sensitisation Programme (RSP) and Travel Fellowship, young doctors travel to the tribal areas and spend time in the clinics. The doctors who have gone through the programme are completely transformed by the experience.

The couple did not ignore the hospital in this process of community development. The hospital expanded to be a thirty-five-bedded secondary care hospital with an ICU, modern investigations and a three-table operation theatre. They now have ten doctors, five of whom are specialists. New projects and innovations like the farmer credit system, the millet centre for excellence, and a fashion tailoring society of tribal women are coming up.

Lalitha and Regi, two specialist doctors who grew up in cities, opted to work for the oppressed in one of the remotest areas of the country, with zero infrastructure, and made a dramatic change not only in health, but in every aspect of their lives, including politics. They empowered them to lead a life with dignity.

> Each of us owe it to the world to do something to make it a better place.

9

The Jailor Who Set His Son Free

Rishiraj Singh, one of the most decorated IPS officers, is a legend. Movies have been made on his heroics. He is from Rajasthan and belongs to Indian Police Service, 1985 Batch, Kerala cadre and was the director general of police (DGP), Kerala. In his last job, he was in charge of prisons.

Post retirement, he is a much sought after motivational speaker. He has been running an anti-drug campaign in schools and colleges. He has written bestselling books on how to bring up children. He is often called 'Mallu Singh'. After retirement, he did not return to Rajasthan. He is much more comfortable among his adoring fans in 'God's Own Country'.

He has brought up his son a lot different from how parents normally do. How did he do it? Rishiraj Singh spoke to me:

'My son, Chatarsal Singh, studied at The Lawrence School, Lovedale, Ooty, from class 4 to 12 (1999–2007). My idea of sending him there was specific: I wanted him to be happy and well-rounded. I wanted him to study, sing, dance, play musical instruments, enjoy sports and make friends.

'We did not want him to be a machine, to be operated through remote switches by me or my wife. I wanted him to be somebody who enjoyed what he was doing. I wanted him to study the things that interested him. We didn't want him to rote learn only for the examinations. We wanted him to discover knowledge.'

Children compulsorily need a sense of happiness every day, which they get by attending to their hobbies, by associating themselves with sports activities, by attending singing and dancing classes, by playing new and varied music instruments, by remaining in constant touch with their friends and thus sharing their inhibitions/difficulties among themselves etc. With this, a child's body releases much required 'dopamine', a neurotransmitter, which brings 'happiness' and contentment on a day-to-day basis in a child's / adolescent's life. Dopamine is called 'the feel-good hormone.'

'Psychologists say that once a child is not allowed to attend to hobbies, sports or musical activities by parents, and instead is lectured and hammered constantly about excelling in studies, with the only objective of getting A+ grade marks, or follow a line in professional career which children don't like, then many children resort to get that very much required "happy hormone" by indulging in drug consumption, smoking, vaping or consuming alcohol. Out of sheer sense of neglect or no respect being given to their feelings or their parents not listening to what they want to do in life, many adolescents commit suicide (In India, 12,000 children below the age of eighteen committed suicide in 2022: that is more than one suicide every hour) or run away from home (In India, 65,000 every year: that is every eight minute a child runs away). We see these tragedies unfolding in the society on regular basis.

'As a parent, I thought let him be happy on a day-to-day basis and encouraged him to do whatever he liked. I just prayed that he be happy, through all legitimate means and not through illegal ways.

'He didn't disappoint me. He played for his school football team, he learnt guitar, he sang songs with friends on annual days, he developed amazing friendship with most of his classmates, was good in horse riding and led his school's band in final day's parade.

'Nevertheless, he was an average student in studies, scoring around 60 per cent or so every year. He learnt manners, imbibed a sense of values and the importance of discipline in life.

'Every time I met his teachers, they would say that he was a very good human being and that if he studied a little more, he would have got good marks. But I never advised him to score more marks at the expense of his hobbies and sports, which he was immensely fond of. I found that he was always happy and contented; that is all as parents we wanted too. When I was the superintendent of police in Kottayam, the government of Kerala had come out with a scheme of encouraging officers to buy a desktop computer, at an interest-free loan of ₹45,000. I bought one for him. He had developed immense interest in animation since he was an eight-year-old. My son got hooked on to the computer and somehow on his own started making pictures/caricatures on it. Later, he took online admission at 'Toonz studio', situated at Techno Park, Trivandrum, and got his first certification in animation. Toonz certification was his passport to his first independent job at London in 2016.

'He made it clear to me that he was not interested in studies and he also told us that he would not go to a college. All he requested was to arrange for a diploma course in animation in any reasonably good animation institution/academy.

'Since I didn't know much about animation institutions situated abroad, I again took help from Jai Kumar, CEO of Toonz Animation, Techno Park; he suggested a reasonably good animation academy in Vancouver, Canada. I took an education loan and he was in Vancouver for two years.

'He came back after completing his diploma studies as the 2008 financial crisis compelled Canadian government to withdraw automatic two year stay in that country, in continuation of two years' diploma course. He applied for a job in a very small studio in Mumbai, for a small remuneration. After six months or so, he applied for a job at Prana animation studio in Mumbai, again on a modest remuneration. At that time, there was a Hollywood animation studio called DreamWorks Animation at Whitefield in Bangalore. DreamWorks Animation studio was the maker of famous movies like *Kung Fu Panda* and *How to Train Your Dragon*. He applied for a job there; they liked his work and hired him. As per their policy at that time, the studio would send a couple of their artists to their London studio to make animated films. In 2016, he was sent to the London studio. From then, there was no looking back for him. After spending some time at DreamWorks Animation, he worked at Studio Weta, owned by Peter Jackson (director of the *Lord of the Rings* trilogy), and other studios at Sydney, Xiamen and Vancouver and worked there till 2022.

'He has been working as a permanent animator at Walt Disney Studios in Los Angeles since March 2022.

'His best animated films, made along with his team, are: *Tinkerbell: The Pirate Fairy*, *Tinkerbell: Legend of the Never Beast*, *Wish Dragon*, *Peter Rabbit 2*, *DC League of Super-Pets* and *Strange World*.

'New theories in adolescent psychology say that talent and genius are overrated. By these alone, one cannot go much far. It is chasing one's dream, constant hard work and able support given by parents, teachers and mentors that help children to achieve their target. Keeping one's passion alive in whatever they do is the key.

'A parent's role in raising their children must be limited to two aspects only: First, encourage them to go in the direction they want to go. They should not impose on them a career they are not interested in. Second, provide children the best of professional education/help.'

What a way to bring up your son, Durgeshawari and Rishi.

> Give your children the freedom to grow.

10

Blood vs Belief

I WAS THE DEPUTY secretary of the School Education Department, Kerala, from 1983 to 1985. I had a small room in the corner of the Secretariat. My stenographer and peon also sat in the same room. It also used to double up as the lunch room for the junior IAS officers in the secretariat. We used to bring packed lunch from home and share the goodies. Jose Cyriac, coming from an aristocratic family, always had chicken. Prabhakaran and Chandran used to bring mostly vegetarian stuff.

I travelled by bus from home to the secretariat. My stenographer and peon also used to travel by the same bus. I almost never got a seat. With the lunchbox in one hand, it was a tough task keeping the balance. There was no danger of falling off as the bus used to be packed with officegoers. I don't think any IAS officer travels by bus any more. As the land revenue commissioner, I ensured that even trainee IAS officers had decent vehicles and a place to stay.

One day, the Director of School Education dropped in at my office with a letter. The contents of the letter were this: some students in a school in Trivandrum refused to sing the national anthem, despite repeated warnings. Their parents were summoned by the school authorities who tried to persuade the parents to instruct their children to sing the national anthem. The parents endorsed the defiance of their children. They said that according to their religion they cannot pay obeisance to any other entity other than Jehovah, who was their God. They said that they would pull out their children if the government persisted.

I was of the opinion that all Indians, especially children, should sing the national anthem as it instils in them a sense of commitment to the country. I prepared a lengthy note in support of my argument, and I discussed the issue with the secretary, J. Lalithambika, and the minister T.M. Jacob. Both of them endorsed my view. I issued orders to the Director of School Education accordingly. They communicated it to the school. Still the students involved refused to sing. They refused to come to the school when the heat was turned on them.

The parents of the children filed a writ petition in the High Court of Kerala with the request to quash the government order. They argued that they were law-abiding citizens but would not sing the national anthem as it involved paying obeisance to the country. They were willing to pay obeisance only to Jehovah. The orders of the government went against the constitutional provision under which they had the right to practice their religion. I was present in the High Court during the argument. The members of Jehovah's Witness engaged some top lawyers of the country to argue the case. The High Court upheld my order. The parents appealed to the Supreme Court of India. Chief Justice Chinnappa Reddy and brother judge struck down my order.[1] They said that it was sufficient to stand with respect during the singing of the national anthem; they need not sing. Forcing them to sing would be a violation of their constitutional rights.

I could not but feel dissatisfied with the order and felt that it laid down an incorrect precedent.

Many years later, the issue popped up in the Supreme Court again. The issue was whether national anthem should be played in movie theatres. The Supreme Court initially ordered that national anthem must be played and everybody should stand up. This was enforced for some time. Later the Supreme court revised its order and ruled that national anthem need not be played in movie halls. I think the court was right. People were too busy with their popcorns to be bothered.

My second battle with the Jehovah's witness was when I was the district collector of Kottayam, 1988–1991. Two young men met me in the office with a representation that a two-and-a-half-year-old boy was dying in their village, and his parents were not treating the child as they were Jehovah's witnesses. The doctor had advised blood transfusion. According to Jehovah's witnesses, blood transfusion was banned. I didn't know why these young men came to me with the representation. There was no law empowering me to take any action. But I couldn't let a child die. I called my personal assistant and dictated the following letter to the station house officer (SHO) of the police station: 'Irrespective of the religious beliefs of the parents, this child has the right to live. Take the child into custody and get him treated at the Government Medical College, Kottayam.' The police took the child into custody forcefully and took him to the Medical College. The doctors gave him blood transfusion and the child was saved.

Two weeks later, a battery of lawyers came to my office and gave me copy of the 1000-page writ petition they had filed against me in Kerala High Court. They have an ongoing battle in courts worldwide on the same issue. In some cases, they had won and in some they had lost. But the law was not settled. All these cases were mentioned in detail in the writ. The advocate general would defend the case on behalf of the government. He asked me to send a draft affidavit with para wise comments on the writ petition. In reply, I sent copy of the three-line directive I had sent to the police. He called me: 'They have filed a 1000-page writ and you are sending me a copy of a three-line letter. This won't do.

You need to refute para by para the averments in the writ.' I told him: 'There is no law which empowers me to do what I did. All the defence I have is in my three-line letter. I have nothing to say beyond that'. On the request of the advocate general, I was summoned by the court. I appeared before His Lordship. The advocate general was present. But he didn't say much. He said that the person who issued the orders would be the better person to defend the case. The judge turned towards me. I was questioned for almost an hour. They wanted to know under what law I issued the orders. I said that there was no law, except that as the representative of the Sovereign, it was my duty to protect the right of the child to live. The lawyer for the petitioner argued for almost two days, citing global judicial antecedents. The High Court pronounced the judgement, upholding what I did. I was greatly relieved because I strongly believed that what I did was right, even though nothing in the law gave me the authority to do it. I believe that persons posted in responsible positions must interpret law to protect human life and dignity. That is precisely why the IAS was created, so that members of the service do not just throw the rule book on hapless citizens.

I never broke the law to help the rich. They would get justice in the normal course. But I would break the law a million times to help the poor. And I would write a detailed note on why I chose to interpret the law to benefit the voiceless.

> Do not throw the rule book on the hapless citizen. Interpret law to uphold human life and liberty.

11

With Them They Brought Light

One and a half billion people of India owed more to twelve men than we owed to anybody else in 2023. These men, called 'rat hole miners', moved a mountain to rescue forty-one tunnel construction workers who were trapped in the Silkyara–Barkot tunnel in Uttarakhand, after a portion of the tunnel they were working on collapsed on 12 November 2023. We had not heard the names of any of these 'rat hole miners' before, and a week later, nobody remembered their names any more. A cricket and Bollywood obsessed nation has more important things to bother about than to remember these rat hole miners.

I am putting down the name of the twelve for posterity: Munna Qureshi, Monu Kumar, Feroz Qureshi, Nasir Khan, Jatin Kashyap, Devender Kumar, Wakeel Hassan, Irshad Ansari, Rashid Ansari, Naseem Malik, Saurabh, Ankur.[1]

We do not even know the surnames of some of these people.

On a normal working day, they earn ₹300–400 a day for a ten-hour shift. Yet, they refused to accept any remuneration for doing such an incredible job. They said that they were just doing their job for fellow human beings. They displayed no sense of entitlement.

The seventeen-day ordeal of the forty-one tunnel workers started on 12 November 2023, on Diwali, the biggest Indian festival. A portion of the 4.5 kilometres long, under-construction tunnel collapsed and trapped the workers inside. Fortunately, the power cable didn't snap. A 4-inch supply line also was not damaged. Through this they were able to send food and medicines and pump oxygen into the trapped area from the very next day.

Over the course of a few days, an 'all of government' approach took shape. The prime minister's principal secretary, P.K. Mishra, was there to coordinate the efforts.

Two days later, on 14 November, horizontal drilling to create an escape passage began. But it did not make much progress as the machine did not have enough thrust. An advanced augur machine was flown in from Hyderabad in a military aircraft. Meanwhile, five independent paths were designed to be pursued to the trapped tunnel, not being too sure which would eventually succeed. Globally renowned experts were called in to advice and assist.

On 16 November, the augur machine started drilling 900 mm steel pipes through the debris. On 20 November, a 6-inch pipe was inserted and through this they sent in a camera, which captured the visuals of the trapped workers. Cooked food began to be sent through this pipe. Constant communication was maintained with the trapped workers to keep their morale high. Once the workers knew that effort was underway to rescue them, they worked out a daily routine of yoga, playing cards and storytelling. They all had plenty of autobiographical stories to tell. They bonded. Meanwhile, drilling continued from five independent routes. By the 22nd, the augur machine had drilled 45 metres into the debris. It broke down a few times, but they were able to get it back to work. But on the 24th, the blades of the machine broke and got stuck in the tunnel. This was a huge setback. Some experts talked about getting them rescued only around Christmas.

The nation was in complete disbelief. That's when somebody brilliantly thought about getting 'rat hole miners' involved and a company called Trenchless Engineering

Services, based in Delhi, provided the 'rat hole miners'. 'Rat hole mining' has been banned in the country due to the danger to human life. It is a procedure to extract coal from mountains. They dig a tiny hole, enter through that, burrow through like a rat, throw back the soil as they dig and reach the coal deposit. Once they reach the coal deposit, they branch off like an octopus into various directions. Miners descend using ropes and sleek ladders. From there they extract coal and send it up through tiny carts. They operate like rats. This is how coal was being extracted in many parts of the North East, especially Meghalaya. Rat hole miners had to be lean, thin and short to be able to do this. Many died in these mines due to asphyxiation and tunnel collapse, before the National Green Tribunal enforced the ban. Still many people are involved in illegal mining.

Devendra, one of the miners, talked about how they did it: 'We can squat on our haunches and rest our body weight on our toes for three hours at a stretch, with our bodies folded as much as possible, to adjust to the space where we are working. We can work like this in as little space as two feet and that is what we did inside the pipe at Silkyara tunnel to reach the blocked portion. We are called rat hole miners but even rats cannot stand or sit like this for three hours at a stretch. We held the drilling machine right in front of us, vertical to our chest, with the heavier part where its motor is fitted, touching the right side of our chest.'[2]

When experts were talking about weeks to dig through the rest, these miners dug through the last 10 metres in less than twenty-four hours to reach the trapped workers on 28 November. There was such jubilation among the workers when they saw these men.

Munna Qureshi was the first rat hole miner to reach them. All the trapped workers came out on their own through the narrow pipe. There was no need to use stretchers. 'The trapped workers hugged us and said that we were godsent. We are also labourers like them, but never had I imagined that I would be saving so many people. I have only studied till class 5 and never thought that I would become a celebrated figure one day,' said Nassir Khan.[3]

How did the rat hole miners do it? It is a miracle and a mystery only they can unravel. We, small mortals with feet of clay, will never get to know how they do it and what drives them.

President Murmu said: 'The nation salutes the workers' resilience and remains grateful to them for building critical infrastructure, even at great personal risk.'[4]

Prime Minister Modi said: 'The success of the rescue operation of our brothers in Uttarakhand is making everyone emotional. The rat hole miners did an incredible job. I want to say a big thank you on behalf of the nation. I want to say to the friends who were trapped in the tunnel that their courage and patience is inspiring everyone.'[5] He also told Gabbar Singh Nego, the tunnel foreman who led the trapped workers in the tunnel for seventeen days: 'You can be a lead case study for universities on how to lead people in a crisis.'

Minister for Roads and Transport, Nitin Gadkari, said: 'This was a well-coordinated effort by multiple agencies, marking one of the most significant rescue operations in recent years. I express my gratitude to each agency and individual involved in it.'[6]

Corporate leader Anand Mahindra said: 'And after all the sophisticated drilling equipment, it's the humble rat hole miners who made the vital breakthrough. It's a heartwarming reminder that at the end of the day, heroism is most often a case of individual effort and sacrifice.'[7]

Congress leader Jairam Ramesh said: 'The entire country salutes the remarkable resilience and fortitude of the workers. The nation also applauds the dedication, skill and perseverance of the entire rescue team.'

A bunch of daring workers did the extraordinary which even the latest technology could not do.

> Crisis requires thinking out of the box.

12

Surrogate Mother in Khaki

I WAS DEEPLY MOVED by a photograph in a newspaper of a lady police officer, Ani Shiva, breastfeeding a kid. It was not front-page news but prominent enough.

What is so fascinating about a lady police officer breastfeeding a kid at a police station? Two things: First, it was not her kid whom she was breastfeeding. Second, it was not even a friend's or neighbours' kid. It was a guest worker's four-month-old baby from Jharkhand (migrant workers are called 'guest workers' in Kerala).

Ani Shiva received a call from the general hospital in Cochin that a lady was admitted to the ICU of the hospital and that her four kids, including the four-month-old baby, had nobody to take care of them. The father of the kids was in jail. The family was originally from Jharkhand, about 3000 kilometres away from Cochin, and they had come to Kerala as guest workers. There are approximately three million guest workers in Kerala, mostly from Bihar, West Bengal, Jharkhand, Chhattisgarh and Odisha. They draw very high wages in Kerala and are treated well. Once in a while, one hears about atrocities being committed on these guest workers. However, prompt action is taken to bring the culprits to book as the media takes up all those cases.

When Ani Shiva received the call at the police station, she rushed to the general hospital. She was informed by the hospital superintendent that since the children had nowhere to go, the police should make necessary arrangement. Ani could not think of any place where she could entrust the children with. So she took them to the police station. The baby girl would not stop crying. Since Ani was the mother of a nine-month-old who was still being breastfed, she immediately knew what the problem was: the baby was hungry. She took the baby to the women police officers' room and breastfed the baby. The baby stopped crying and drank to her heart's fill. She smiled. It was such an expression of gratitude. Fellow lady officers clicked the picture on their mobiles and Ani Shiva became a huge hero in print and on social media.

Ani Shiva, from Vaikom, had returned to duty only three months ago after maternity leave. Her nine-month-old baby would be thrilled and proud when she grows up, hearing stories of her mother feeding a stranger's baby.

On the same day, in Surat, a town about 1700 kilometres away from Cochin, police constable Veerabhai Rabari, was involved in a heroic act of saving a senior citizen from being crushed under a train. Veerabhai was on patrol duty at Vapi police station. Shyamal, a sixty-five-year-old man, accompanied by his son, was waiting to board the train from platform number two. Suddenly it was announced that the train would arrive on platform number one. Shyamal and his son panicked. Instead of using the overbridge to change platforms, they decided to get down to the tracks and cross over, as many commuters in India do.

Shyamal's son managed to cross the track. Shyamal was still crossing when the Bandra–Surat Intercity Express entered the platform. The loco pilot applied brakes but the train could not be stopped. Veerabhai noticed it. He jumped down onto the track and dragged Shyamal out of the way. The train missed them by a split second. Passengers who witnessed the heroics were amazed at what Veerabhai did and applauded him. When asked how he had the guts to do what he did, this is what he said: 'I was confident that if I acted with speed, I could pull the elderly man and save his life.' A video of the act went viral on social media.

Railway GRP Superintendent of Police Sarojini Kumari said: 'After getting the CCTV camera footage of the incident, we called up Veerabhai and congratulated him. Our policeman has put his life in danger and saved the life of a passenger. We will, in the coming days, felicitate him and also write to the Director General of Police recommending him for bravery award.'

Both Anni Shiva and Veerabhai are just ordinary people working in the police department. They showed incredible sensitivity and courage to do what they did. For Anni Shiva, it didn't matter that it was an unknown child – a child was a child. For Veerabhai, it didn't matter that he didn't know Shyamal. The fact that it was another human being was good enough.

Think beyond oneself.

13

Tessy Thomas: India's Missile Woman

INDIA BECAME A NUCLEAR power in 1999, as it was in that year that we dared to weaponise our nuclear capability. We had the capability even during Indira Gandhi's regime. Even a strong prime minister like Mrs Gandhi did not take it forward. She was scared what the world nuclear powers would do in retaliation. Prime Minister Vajpayee had the courage to take the leap.

Finally, we had the weapon, but we did not have the delivery system. Nobody delivers a nuclear bomb in an aircraft any more, as was done in Hiroshima and Nagasaki. We needed short, medium and long-range missiles, capable of being nuclear tipped. This is what Tessy and her team at the Defence Research and Development Organisation (DRDO) did. They developed the Agni series, which have the capability to strike anywhere in the world.

Tessy was born in Thyparambil house, Thathampally, in Alleppey, Kerala, as the fourth child of Mr T. J. Thomas and Thresiamma Thomas. She studied at the local school, St Michael's, till class 4 and then shifted to St Joseph's Girls High School at Alleppey. She never missed study tours and picnics conducted by the school. On one such occasion, she got the opportunity to visit the Thumba rocket launching station at Trivandrum, where sounding rockets were launched by ISRO. This ignited her interest in aerospace.

She used to wonder how aircrafts flew so high and was amazed at seeing the trail of smoke coming out of the jet planes. She was fascinated seeing the stars in the sky shining like tiny dots. She would enjoy walking in the night, looking at the sky, at the stars and the moon and would always feel that she was walking along with the moon till she reached home. She was curious to know all about space, earth's rotation and other planets.

Her father had a paralytic stroke when she was thirteen. It was traumatic for her and a tough time for her family. But she never gave up on studies and she knew that it was possibly the only salvation. She did her pre-degree from St Joseph's Women's College, Alleppey, and secured good marks and got admitted at Government Engineering College, Thrissur, for electrical engineering. The turning point in her life was when, after graduation, she chanced to see an advertisement in the daily newspaper about a postgraduate degree course in missile systems being offered by Pune University, at the Institute of Armament Technology, presently known as Defence Institute of Advanced Technology (DIAT). She applied and was selected as one among the ten students from across the country. Studying about missile technology gave her insights into missile applications and the importance of such systems in defence.

Early in her career, Tessy joined the DIAT, DRDO, as a faculty member in guided missiles department. She later got the opportunity to join the Defence Research and Development Laboratory (DRDL), Hyderabad, in 1988, where Dr A.P.J. Abdul Kalam was the Director of the laboratory. She remembers every moment she spent with Dr Kalam; he became her mentor. The second turning point in her career was when Dr Kalam advised her to join the navigation and guidance group. She obtained an MBA and a PhD while in service.

She got married to Lt Saroj Kumar Patel, an officer in the Indian Navy, in 1989 and they were blessed with a son, Tejas, named after the fighter plane project of India. Along with her hectic schedules at DRDO and balancing all odds of career and personal life, she was able to guide her son to take up engineering and finish his degree from Vellore Institute of Technology, Vellore.

Tessy was associated with the Agni programme right from its developmental stage. She has designed the guidance scheme for long range missile systems. An energy management guidance scheme was designed and developed for the first time in the country for an all-solid propelled long-range system, for which she was conferred with the Agni self-reliance award in 2001. She has been the mission designer for India's prestigious Agni missile systems, with a range capability from 300 kilometres to 5000 kilometres, comprising of the AGNI series (AGNI 1–5 and its variants) and contributed towards the successful flight tests of more than fifty missions.

There were many heartbreaking failures on the way. There were sleepless nights. But she bounced back. With a positive mindset, she always inspired her team members to take steps to learn and improve, till a scientific solution was found. Being the first woman to lead a missile project in India, she is an epitome of perseverance, team work and leadership. In her career spanning more than thirty-six years, she has contributed to various fields such as guidance, control, inertial navigation, trajectory simulation and mission design. She led a major project, AGNI-4, as the project director for the state-of-art system, incorporating many new technologies for the first time. The rocket motor casing with the composite materials, with carbon fibre as raw material, was used for the first time in the country. She was also the mission project director for the long-range AGNI-5 system and designed three stages of guidance scheme for achieving high impact accuracies.

As director of Advanced Systems Laboratory, DRDO, she held multi-dimensional roles and responsibilities and led the development of indigenous, strategic missiles and infrastructure. In 2018, she was appointed as the Director General Aeronautical Systems Cluster Laboratories, responsible for designing and developing state-of-the-art UAVs, Manned and Unmanned aircrafts, aero-gas turbine engines, airborne surveillance systems, technologies and systems related to parachute for the armed forces. Under her guidance, the subsonic cruise missile, Nirbhay, was flight tested successfully, leading to deployment of multiple cruise missiles with long range land attack capability. Under her guidance, Light Combat Aircraft (LCA) Tejas had its final operational clearance for induction to Indian Air Force, leading to production of LCA by Hindustan Aeronautics Limited (HAL).

Tessy is a recipient of several prestigious awards and honours, including Lal Bahadur Shastri National award for Excellence in Public Administration Academics and Management (2012).

DRDO has taken off on the Agni project, where Tessy had left it.

On 11 March 2024, India tested an AGNI-5 missile with Multiple Independently Targeted Re-entry Vehicle (MIRV), joining a small group of countries with the capability. This allows multiple war heads to be loaded on a single missile, which can strike at multiple targets. This would make it possible to penetrate through missile defence systems of the enemy and strike at the targets as it would be difficult to track and intercept. It has a range of over 5000 kilometres, making it an Intercontinental Ballistic Missile.

Tessy, coming from a small-time town, having done her schooling in a local school and engineering from a local engineering college, has been instrumental in critical innovations for the defence of the country.

> Aim for the stars and you will get somewhere near there.

14

Kids, Don't Be Photocopies

FROM THE TIME KIDS are born, the biggest effort of the parents is to make them photocopies of themselves. Sad part is, many kids themselves think that it is a good idea. We often hear kids say: 'I want to be like my father/mother.' And sadly, often they succeed.

How does one make photocopies? At the age of three, parents scout for the best nursery school in town. Out of 500 kids who apply, maybe 100 get shortlisted for interview. Straightaway, 400 kids are told that they are losers. Imagine a kid being put to test at the age of three. In fact, it is a bigger test for the parents. They have sleepless nights. Then there is the interview, which can be quite tough for the young ones. It is again another period of nerve-racking tension, till the final admission list is out. After the torturous ordeal, when the list is published, possibly 50 get selected. At the age of three, 450 out of the 500 applicants are told that they are hopeless. The parents are quick to condemn their children: 'You are useless. You could not even get through the nursery class admission.'

Once admitted, what are they taught, from nursery school onwards? They are taught rigorously the most insane things a kid should never be learning. Our education system destroys all the creativity in a child. It destroys the inner soul.

One of my favourite songs, which I listen to at least once a week is Pink Floyd's 'Brick in the Wall'. In fact, when I speak in schools and colleges, I request the principals to start the day with that song. The lyrics go like this:

We don't need no education
We don't need no thought control
No dark sarcasm in the classroom
Teacher, leave them kids alone
Hey teacher,
Leave them kids alone
All in all, just another brick in the wall.

This is what education is today. The objective is to convert these brilliant kids into uniform bricks, photocopies, so that everybody thinks and behaves the same way. It then becomes easy for those in power to control the society.

When I was the secretary of higher education, the government of Kerala organised a reception at VJT Hall in Thiruvananthapuram for the girl who secured the first rank in the Higher Secondary Examination from Kerala. It was a grand function, attended by the chief minister. The media was there to cover the brilliant achievement of the biggest genius of the state. After the function was over, I asked her: 'What are you going to do with your life?' She was shocked. Nobody had asked her the question, not her parents, not her teachers, not her friends. She thought for a long time and responded: 'I will ask my mother and tell you.' The most 'brilliant' seventeen-year-old needed to ask her mother what she wanted to do with her life. This is what most of the products of our educational system are: perfect bricks. She did not even miss a comma from what was taught. That was the secret of being the topper: vomit out on the answer sheet whatever the teacher or instructor dictated in the classroom. You don't need to comprehend what is dictated. Go to tuition teachers, repeat and repeat. I can understand somebody getting 100 per cent in maths. But it beats my logic as to how somebody can score 100 per cent in History and English literature. They can, because there is a formula.

We tell our kids: 'You look at that kid. They are so smart. Why can't you be like them?' I used to tell my kids: 'Nobody like you has ever existed and will ever exist. You are unique. Don't ever want to be like me or your mother. Don't ever want to be like somebody else. Be yourself. Whatever you want to be is fine for me.' My sons were kicked out of Don Bosco School, Delhi, because they were considered 'not up to the mark'. I put them in Bluebells School, East of Kailash. There, my younger son, Adarsh, again got into trouble. He was taken by the class teacher to the principal, with the complaint that he was painting and scribbling in textbooks and homework books. Any other principal might have told Adarsh to bring his parents the next day to meet her. One could expect fireworks. But Principal Suman Kumar told him: 'Your classroom walls are white, paint them; when you finish your classroom, paint the entire school.' My son came home and told me: 'Appa, my principal seems to be crazy like you; she told me to paint the entire school. Can I be a painter?' I said: 'Do whatever you want.' We went to Lajpat Nagar and bought canvases that evening. Adarsh was eight. At eleven, Adarsh had his first solo exhibition, inaugurated by the famous Anjalie Ela Menon and became the youngest independent tax payer in India, selling paintings. In fact, Principal Suman Kumar organised the exhibition. At twelve, he had a solo exhibition at the Lalit Kala Academy. At thirteen, his global exhibition in Delhi, at India Habitat Centre, was inaugurated by the president of India, K.R. Narayanan. It travelled from Delhi to London, New York and Washington DC. He got to meet Nelson Mandela twice, and gifted him his paintings. I, as the parent, had the privilege to accompany my son. What an honour to meet one of the greatest persons in the history of the world. By the time he completed school, he had got admission into ten of the best fine art schools in the US. He took up painting. At thirty, Adarsh was in the list of fifty biggest philanthropists. My elder son, Akash, was good at cricket and was selected to join Madan Lal Academy of Cricket. He had also got admission into engineering. He asked me: 'What do you think I should pursue?' I told him: 'Son, it's your choice.' He went into engineering. He is a well-read and compassionate young man. Neither of them is a photocopy. Thank God.

Most parents want their children to be doctors or engineers. Why? Because that is where the big money is. Some get in due to commitment. What is the route to get there? The route is generally through the killing fields of Kota, in Rajasthan. That is where the coaching factories are located. Till a few years ago, only those who passed class 10 used to go to Kota. Now many parents send their kids to Kota, when they get into middle school, at the age of thirteen or fourteen, because they believe that the early bird catches the worm. This is when the persecution of the innocents begins. These teenagers, bubbling with life, when they need parental care most, are put into a cage, where all that they do is sit at their desk for the whole day and study and study and study. They don't talk to anyone. They do not smile at anyone. They do not socialise. They do no sports. They do not exercise. They carry the burden of the dream of their parents that they have to get into IITs or into the most prestigious medical colleges. Nobody ever asked these kids whether they wanted to be engineers or doctors. Their parents decided. Nobody cared to find out whether they had the aptitude. Kota has its well-oiled photocopying machines. Thousands get enrolled there. The burnout is so quick. There are endless tests and examinations. If you fall behind, they grill you. You are shamed before the whole class. Teachers have no time to look for signs of distress. Nobody cares to talk to them. They are left with no options. There were ninety-five suicides in Kota between 2015 and 2022. There were no suicides in Kota in 2020 and 2021 as the coaching centres were closed during the Covid-19 pandemic.

Some make it to IITs and elite medical colleges. Those who don't make it, go home with incurable scars. Their parents stamp them as useless. Recently, the government of India issued regulations to control the killer factories of Kota. Many of them will find ways to get around the regulations.

The government came out with a National Education Policy (NEP) in July 2020. I was a member of the drafting committee till I became a union minister. It has some brilliant ideas. The key take is don't let kids be photocopies; let them discover knowledge; let them experiment. It was easy to write the document. However, it is a big task to make it real. CBSE, ISC, ICSE and UGC are trying desperately to bring their curriculum in line with the NEP. They have a tough job in hand. It is not just about the curriculum; it is about the mindset. First of all, we need to educate the parents; then, we need to change the mindset of teachers. Both of these are complicated task.

We need to bring up children who are able to think for themselves, take a stand and have the courage to pursue their own dreams, so that we create a better world. There is no point in becoming a photocopy.

> Never be like anybody else. Be yourself. Don't ape. Think for yourself and do things in your own way.

15

Sujatha and the Power of Self-Help Groups

Mohan was an agricultural labourer, who now lay paralysed from the waist down after he fell from a jackfruit tree in his compound. He was now a bundle of bones. Sujatha, his wife, was a domestic help before Mohan had the accident. They were in deep debt after prolonged treatment. He needed her around and so she stopped working. They had two school-going children. They were almost at the point of starvation. Sujatha hardly slept. When she woke up from her half slumber, her only thought was how to end her life. She didn't see any purpose in life, since she couldn't even feed her family. That's when a Kudumbashree volunteer dropped in for a chat. That was in 2019. Fast forward to 2024, Sujatha is a community leader with considerable assets and savings. She is excited when she wakes up every morning.

Imagine a self-help group comprising of 4.6 million active women members, who are involved in livelihood activities in the tiny state of Kerala! It is the largest such group anywhere in the world. It has created millions of jobs, created thousands of micro enterprises, lent over ₹24,000 crore directly and facilitated bank loans worth another ₹26,000 crore. It is something worth emulating anywhere in the world, especially in developing countries.

Atal Bihari Vajpayee, the then prime minister of India, launched Kudumbashree at Malappuram on 17 May 1998. The Mission, commonly known as Kudumbashree (meaning 'prosperity of the family'), is a society registered under the Travancore Kochi Literary, Scientific and Charitable Societies Act, 1955.

The first project director was T.K. Jose. Prior to that assignment, he was the district collector of Malappuram, Kerala. An outstanding officer with exceptional abilities, he set the ball rolling. Later, Sarada Muraleedharan, Harikishore and Jafar Malik, all outstanding IAS officers, did a great job.

The mission statement of Kudumbashree is to eradicate absolute poverty in ten years, through concerted community action, under the leadership of local governments, by facilitating organisation of the poor and combining self-help with demand-led convergence of available services and resources to tackle the multiple dimensions and manifestations of poverty, holistically.

Kudumbashree, a community-based organization (CBO), is a three-tier structure of poor women, with neighbourhood groups (NHGs) at the grassroot level, the federation of which at the panchayat ward level is called an area development society (ADS) and at the panchayat level it is called a community development society (CDS). The CBOs have their own byelaw, and elections are conducted as envisaged in the byelaws.

Kudumbashree works on the principle of bottom-up approach, wherein the requirements of the community are assessed by them and helps the local governments to integrate the community requirements in their annual plan. The CBOs of the poor was visualised as partners to local governments, not as parallel to them.

The CBOs prepare their demand plan, known as CDS demand plan (the demand is generated and prepared at the NHG level and consolidated at ADS and CDS level), which is presented to the Evaluation Committee (the panchayat president as its chairman, with representation of all transferred line departments, banks and community), to integrate the demand with the panchayat plan and department plans. Byelaws ensure the rights of the community in local planning and participation in development plans (participation in Gram/Ward Sabha).

The Mission focuses on the economic empowerment of women, by encouraging micro finance, livelihood activities (wage and self-employment), social empowerment through inclusion, providing opportunities for leadership positions, by sensitising them to their basic rights and capacity building to claim these rights.

Today, Kudumbashree is one of the biggest women's networks in the world, with more than 4.6 million women in the Kudumbashree network, through 3,09,667 NHGs.

The Mission, over a period of time, has changed its strategy from mere poverty reduction to women empowerment through experimentation, assessing the factors contributing to poverty and the ways and means to address them. The Mission addresses women, children and the marginalised and their requirements. The Mission encourages small micro finance activities among NHGs, to promote small savings and internal lending among women, availing linkage loan with the support of thrift to avoid money lenders; it also promotes self-employment as a means of livelihood in production, service sector, animal husbandry and farming; they support the marginalised like destitute, differentially abled, scheduled castes, children of members of NHGs; there are programmes to support the needy, like street vendors (social entitlements and livelihood), landless and homeless.

Hundreds of restaurants were set up, where subsidised meals were being provided to the needy, at ₹20, and the state government was providing ₹10 as subsidy. Since the subsidy was not being paid on time, many of these hotels have sadly closed down.

Kudumbashree Initiative for Business Solutions (KIBS), a society registered under the Travancore–Kochi Scientific Charitable Societies Act 1955, formed in 2021, provides services to various institutions such as Kochi Water Metro, IIT Palakkad, Industries Department, Railway Mail Service (RMS), Medical College, Ernakulam, KILA, Thrissur, and PWD rest houses. The majority of employees who got benefited are women and at present 280 employees are working under KIBS.

Kudumbashree is not alone in empowering women. It has been happening across the country. *Down to Earth* writes: 'In India, women self-help groups have been a source of empowerment, fostering economic independence, social stature and community resilience. By pooling resources, providing micro finance opportunities and promoting entrepreneurship, these groups have significantly contributed to the reduction of poverty and demonstrated a successful model of grassroots development ... Today, these groups are regarded as the world's largest microfinance project. As of February 2023, some 8.9 million SHGs have availed ₹2.54 lakh crore as loans ... Notably SHGs's bank repayment is more than 96 per cent, underscoring their credit discipline and reliability.'[1]

Prime Minister Modi said: 'Over a period of time, Self Help Groups will turn into "Nation Help Groups".[2] He also said that eventually every rural household will have one member in the local SHG. He set a target of creating one crore 'lakhpati didis'.

Let's look at some of the SHGs that have been phenomenally successful elsewhere. In 1972, Ela Bhat set up Self Employed Women's Association (SEWA) in Gujarat. Nobody was willing to lend them money. In 1974, SEWA set up the Mahila Sewa Cooperative Bank. Its founding members, 4000 of them, contributed ₹10,000 each as the founding capital. Today, SEWA has 4000 SHGs, 110 cooperative societies, 15 federations of cooperatives and 3 companies. They are all managed by women. It now has operations in 18 states.

Chumur, in Ladakh, is home to the finest pashmina wool in the world. But the producers got very little. The raw material was sent to the neighbouring states, where it was converted to value-added products. In 2017, eight villages organised themselves into SGHs and the 'Looms of Ladakh' collective was born. In 2023, its sales grew to over ₹40 lakh.

Arti Devi Kol became the sarpanch of Bousad Panchayat in Madhya Pradesh, thanks to the SHG she joined in 2020.

In Odisha, SHGs are involved with implementation of government projects. One of the biggest achievements of these SHGs have been the revitalisation of Bhubaneshwar's Nicco Park, which was completely wrecked in the 2019 floods. In Puri, water management is done by SHGs of women. They are called 'jal sathis'. They opened a caffe in 2023, which has been very successful. On the exhortation of the prime minister and the chief minister, 'Millet Cafes' are being opened across Odisha by SHGs.

In Tamil Nadu, one of the most successful programmes have been the 'Amma Canteen', launched in 2013 by the then chief minister Jayalalitha, to provide affordable meals, through the network of SHGs. There are 407 such canteens functioning across the state, employing 4500 women. The numbers are enormous: daily they prepare about 5 million idlis, 1.5 million plates of Pongal, 3 million plates of sambar rice and 1.3 million plates of curd rice. This model has caught up in other states: 'Annapurna Rasoi Yojana' in Rajasthan, 'Deendayal Canteen' in Madhya Pradesh and 'NTR Anna Canteens' in Andhra Pradesh.

In Karnataka, 18,000 women from 2000 SHGs are involved in cleaning up rural and urban areas. The project was started under the National Rural Livelihood Mission and provide solid waste management training to women from low-income families. The project is supported by the state government departments.

Why can't the rest of the country follow these models? Women can earn, which will bring dignity to their lives. It will lead to betterment of the lives of their children.

> Government cannot do everything. When we organise ourselves into self-help groups, we can achieve the impossible. Women collectives can have incredible impact in bringing dignity to women by making them financially independent.

16

Kottayam: India's First 100 Per Cent Literate Town

On 12 June 1989, Kottayam town was declared as the first 100 per cent literate town in India.

The literacy campaign in Kottayam town included fifteen special campaigns, other than literacy, involving all the inhabitants of the city. Some of these were: read more books, green the city, keep the city clean, physical fitness, traffic sense, immunisation, alcoholism and drugs, cancer education, and vegetable cultivation. The intention was to improve the quality of life of every citizen, not just the illiterates.

The Kottayam literacy campaign was not my idea. The project was conceptualised by the National Service Scheme (NSS) of Mahatma Gandhi University, under the leadership of the Vice Chancellor, Mr U.R. Ananthamurthy, a reputed author. I came into the scene when they realised that the best person to coordinate a project of this magnitude would be the district collector, as it required the cooperation of every citizen.

A detailed survey was conducted by the NSS volunteers of the University. They visited every house, talked to every family member, to make sure that every illiterate person was identified. Once we had the figures, we got down to planning how to go about it. We involved everybody at this stage: MP, MLA, Municipal Chairman Mani Abraham, municipal councillors, representatives of all political parties, all the colleges and schools in town, voluntary organisations, authors, journalists and all the newspapers. We wanted everyone, the rich and the poor, to be involved. Before the campaign was launched, we had to sell the idea to the public. I met the editors of all the newspapers and got a commitment that they would set apart minimum of a quarter of a page every day in their newspapers for the campaign. Every newspaper posted an exclusive correspondent to cover the literacy story. We used television and radio to spread the idea.

Their efforts paid off: we got hundreds of volunteers, from all segments of the society, coming forward to teach. Most of the volunteers were from poor families, who had barely completed their school; most of them were unemployed. We set a minimum qualification of class 10 to be a volunteer. Sometimes we made an exception: we had an eight-year-old teaching an eighty-year-old. We also had a considerable number of ladies from elite families enrolling. We made a dirty word 'illiteracy' into a fashionable word. Everybody wanted to be involved with us; nobody wanted to be left out. We had to train these volunteers on exactly what the protocol was.

We decided that we would follow the principle of 'each one teach one'. The rationale for this was simple: in a city like Kottayam, where the literacy rate was already high, people who were illiterate would not come forward in the open, as there was a social stigma attached to it. So, each volunteer was attached to a learner, who had to be taught in the home of the learner, at her/his convenience. Most of the illiterates were homemakers, head load workers or maids. Once they came out of their shells, after the initial reluctance, they were willing to gather at a neighbourhood house to learn together.

'Each one teach one' didn't mean that a volunteer couldn't teach more than one. We had a volunteer, Indulekha, who taught nineteen persons. She was just a class 10 failed, unemployed girl, who lived in the slum, next to the railway track. She went on to win the national youth award from the president of India. Later, the Municipality built a house for her.

After a detailed planning, we decided that if it was to happen, it had to be done on campaign mode, with a time frame. We fixed a target of 100 days. The slogan was: 100 days, 100 per cent literacy.

The vice chancellor was at it the whole day and night. He breathed literacy. Thomas Abraham, the NSS Coordinator was a livewire. He didn't go home for 100 days. He stayed in a tiny room in a lodge. He hardly slept. The heart and soul of the entire campaign were the 32 NSS volunteers from the University. They were assigned geographical areas, for which the buck stopped with them. At the end of the campaign, they all emerged as completely transformed entities. Most of them used these campaign strategies in their lives and have been hugely successful. Nothing could have taught them anything better, not even an internship in the most valued multinational corporation.

I set apart half a day exclusively for the campaign, every day. I decided that I would teach two persons in the slum, next to the railway track. My reason for doing so was simple: nobody else should say that they were too busy to volunteer. If the collector could find time, anybody else could fine time. This had incredible impact. A lot of government employees, teachers, businessmen and college students came forward. K.M. Mathew, the editor of Vanitha magazine, and his wife, the chief editor of Malayala Manorama newspaper, drove down in her Premier Padmini to a remote corner of the city to teach. This had huge impact. Kottayam breathed and lived literacy. The only conversation even in upper middle-class clubs was literacy.

We met for a daily assessment of the progress every day late at night, after the day's assignment was over. There were plenty of things going wrong, even after the detailed planning. We made sure that these were discussed and corrective measures taken every day.

Halfway into the campaign, we still had 118 persons, who still had not started learning. Of these, 91 persons were incapable of learning, due to physical and mental challenges and alcoholism. We had persuaded over a 100 drug addicts to give up addiction and start learning through expert counselling. We succeeded with a lot of alcoholics, again with expert intervention. So, we were left with 27 persons, to be persuaded. It was decided that the municipal chairman and I would visit all these persons at their homes. We managed to persuade 22 of them. The task of dealing with the rest 5 was left to me. I visited all of them and persuaded 4 of them. That left just Kuttappan as the lone obstacle.

Kuttappan had dropped out of school when he was seven, after the headmaster bashed him up for having a quarrel with a high caste boy. He felt that it was completely unjustified and vowed to God that he would never study. Now he was forty-five. I went to his house and had a long conversation. He wouldn't relent. I told him that I was taking him to the police station. Instead, I took him, along with his wife, to my home, fed them a sumptuous fish curry meal and sweet-talked him into learning.

Kuttappan is just one story. The campaign had thousands of other stories, some exciting, some dull. But each story is an example of determination against all odds.

We did not stop with hundred days. We went on. The NSS volunteers were to be in the wards for six more months. The other volunteers continued their effort and brought up most of the learners to a level where they were able to handle language independently. We had to maintain the enthusiasm of the new literates for at least another six months, to ensure that they were using language as a tool in their day to day lives. We had regular workshops on holidays and held street corner meetings as often as we could. We could not let the flame die even though the declaration was done.

After Kottayam's historic achievement, K.R. Rajan, the district collector of Ernakulam, made his district the first 100 per cent literate district in the country.

Eventually, not just the town, the entire Kottayam district became 100 per cent literate in 1990. We had 14000 volunteers who made it possible. Most of them were women, a good number being teenage girls. It was a demonstration of women's power. Every MLA and panchayat president competed against each other to be the first.

People will ask: what good did literacy do to Kottayam? Plenty. As per Niti Aayog evaluation in 2023, Kottayam is the only 100 per cent zero poverty district in the country. Kottayam is a role model for a lot of things. 100 per cent children are immunised. It has the lowest maternal mortality and infant mortality rates in the country.

The ability to use language is what distinguishes human beings from other animals. India has made immense progress in adult literacy since the Kottayam experiment. However, there is still a long way to go before India becomes fully literate. There is also a wide gender gap in literacy rate. We need to close this gap quickly.

Literacy is the most powerful weapon of the citizen. Adult literacy can be achieved with the collective efforts of the government and the citizen.

17

Empathy in Magic

MAGICIAN GOPINATH MUTHUKAD IS almost in the same league as David Copperfield, the greatest proponent of the mystery of magic on the planet. He won the Merlin award in 2011, the highest honour for a magician. He has done more than 8000 public shows.

For forty-five years, Muthukad's magic has enthralled the world, blending Indian culture, myths and tales untold. Through his illusions, he sheds light on strife, child labour, violence and nature's fragile life. His magic has always had a message.

But his true passion, his noblest deed, is empowering special children and fulfilling their needs. In Thiruvananthapuram, Kerala, he has built the Different Art Centre (DAC), where the magic of impossible dreams took shape. Three hundred children with special needs find solace here through magic and art; they discover their own dreams. What he does is a miracle. I had the privilege to be with his magical children on many occasions.

In 2016, an incident profoundly changed Mr Muthukad. He was performing in Kasaragod. This district was hugely affected by the use of endosulfan, a pesticide used in cashew plantation for almost half a century. Thousands of children were born with physical and cranial deformity. In spite of public outcry, the government was not willing to ban its usage. Finally, an NGO took the fight to the Supreme Court and the court banned the use of the pesticide and ordered payment of compensation to the victims and directed the state to create the necessary infrastructure to take care of those affected. Even a decade after the Supreme Court judgement the victims have not been compensated fully and very little infrastructure has been put in place to take care of those affected. Endosulfan continues to be widely used in this area and the neighbouring districts under some other brand name.

A large number of children affected by endosulfan and their parents were in Muthukad's audience that day in 2016. He witnessed the struggles etched on each face and the deep distress in the hearts of their parents. After the performance he stayed back for a day in the city to interact with the families. He felt deeply devastated by the experience. Most of those affected were from poor families, mostly workers in cashew plantations. They could not go to work as they had to take care of these children 24x7. There were no medical facilities to treat these children. They could not be sent to school as there were no special schools. The livery of misery was written all over. He decided that he was going to do something for these children, and the Magic Academy at Trivandrum embarked on a grand mission to create a world where special children could live with dignity and fend for themselves.

Magic became the medium, the catalyst for change, as these children discovered a world so strange. It was a huge struggle to initiate them into magic as most of them were physically disabled and had limited mental capacity. Magic requires quick thinking and action at lightning speed to be effective in creating the illusion. Patience, coupled with day after day of training for months, brought 'magical change' in their responses. An evaluation by the Child Development Centre revealed the impact Magic Academy had on their physical, social and mental development; this programme brought joy and lifted their spirits. Inspired by the results, Muthukad dreamt bigger.

He set up DAC next to the Magic Academy. He put all his saving into it. He had to buy a large tract of land. Land was extremely expensive in Trivandrum. Besides, it had to be next to the Magic Academy. Cost of land was just a fraction of the total cost of DAC. He had to create a vast infrastructure with residential facilities for 300 children, classrooms and laboratories, performance areas, stages, work area for children of the residents and a million things more. Eventually, he had to sell off the last property his wife owned and they moved to DAC.

He set up seven separate centres at DAC: Beethoven Bungalow for music, Jaleo Mahal for dance, Camile Cascade for magic, India Fort for instrumental music, Angelo for drawing and painting, Different Thought Centre and a Theatre for professional magic show.

Children discover themselves through vocal and instrumental music, dance, theatre, arts and magic in the first five schools. Last two schools are for interaction of the children with the public. Through these, the children find a chance to unleash their potential. The objective is to create empowerment, independence, earn an income to stand on their own feet and to nurture each soul. It involves love and dedication, not only from Muthukad, but also from the hundreds of teachers, supporting staff, parents and the public. Learning centres of DAC hold public performances every day, where thousands flock to see the magic of transformation. Appreciation from the public boosts their confidence incredibly. They get a feeling that they have arrived somewhere, even though a tough journey lies ahead.

They were deeply thrilled when the president of India, Draupadi Murmu, invited them to the Rashtrapati Bhavan, the president's residence, for an interaction in 2022. I had the privilege to accompany them.

DAC also has a centre for training parents of the special children enrolled at DAC. Muthukad realised that instead of whiling away their time, mourning about their children, the parents should be fruitfully occupied, where they would become productive assets of the society. They are taught various skills to produce things required by the local community. Whatever is produced is sold in the DAC outlet and the money goes to the parents.

Muthukad's next venture is 'The International Institute for People with Disabilities', at Kasargod, Kerala. This would focus more specifically on children who are victims of the endosulfan tragedy. Creation of the necessary infrastructure is going on. It will be able to accommodate 1000 special children.

How does a man give up everything he has for somebody else's children? It is not just about money. That is just a fraction of the total effort that goes into the whole project. Each child at DAC is a project in themselves. Muthukad and his family has done it.

> Sometimes you have to give everything away for something much bigger.

18

The Slum Doctor

IN LIFE'S JOURNEY, ONE comes across people who look ordinary but have done extraordinary things with their lives. One such person is Dr Surya, whom I met at India International Centre, Delhi. What makes her extraordinary?

About 7 per cent of all medical graduates from India are working in developed countries, even though there is a shortage of medical doctors in the country, especially postgraduates and super specialists. The temptation to work abroad is strong for both nurses and doctors. They are paid much better abroad and the working conditions are far better. Most of the graduates from the most prestigious institutes go abroad for higher studies and never return. Indian doctors are in big demand, as they are competent. Same with our nurses.

Here is a huge departure from the norm: Dr Surya Kant Suri.

She is not someone who hits the front pages of newspapers; she never did and possibly never will; she never even featured in a page three story. But she is a goddess to many people, in an unknown little corner of Delhi.

Dr Surya, a medical doctor, did a postgraduate degree in obstetrics and gynaecology from one of the most prestigious institutions in India before she went to the Royal College of Gynaecology and Obstetrics, London, for super specialisation. By the time she was completing her course, she had multiple tempting offers from prestigious hospitals in London and India to join them as senior consultant; she could have quoted any price and they would have taken her. Those days, people with such qualifications were rare in India. Let Dr Surya narrate her own story:

'The year was 1970. I was in a plane, coming back home after studying at the Royal College of Gynaecology and Obstetrics in London, in addition to having gained a lot of clinical experience in the field there. I could have stayed back in London, had a roaring practice and a comfortable life. But I had already made up my mind: I wanted to return to my country and serve the poor. Guess what was my first reaction after touching down at Mumbai airport? I bent down and kissed my land, my sail, my India.

'Next was to locate an area to work from. I went to the Servants of People's Society in Lajpat Nagar. I met the President, Ishwar Prasad, and told him of my intentions. He guided me to a place called Madangir, near Saket. I had never visited a slum before. There were mountains of garbage; pigs were roaming around freely; there was poverty all around. I went to the main market; there were a few doctors' 'shops' around, all fake ones. Some IV drip poles were displayed at the reception, to deceive the innocent. Fake they were, but they had lots of patients waiting for 'consultation'. I felt sorry for my country. In my heart I knew that this was going to be the place where I wanted to set up my practice.

'My friends, fellow doctors and relatives were all shocked. "How can you work here in the slum, with all your knowledge and degree from London? Even Indian postgraduates or graduate medical practitioners would not go anywhere near that. You have wasted time, effort and money studying so much if you were going to work in the slum. You will die of some infection." Everyone I knew dissuaded me. When I started working from Madangir, my relatives and friends would not mention in social gatherings the locality where I was working. They were ashamed of where I was working.

Some would chide me in public. They got the best hospitals in Delhi to call me up with tempting offers. But that was not my goal.

'Forty years later, I am working in the same area. I have relished every day of my existence. God alone knows how many people have passed through my hands. I have had so much of blessings from them. One resident, I never forget, a female daily wage worker, came to me for fertility treatment. I treated her and she became pregnant. Guess what? She brought a garland of ₹1 notes, put it around my neck and fell on my feet. ₹1 was the highest denomination currency she ever had. It was deeply touching. Old patients coming and touching my feet in gratitude is so common. I feel deeply embarrassed when they do that, but that is their only way to express their happiness. They have no money.

'My life has been so incredibly blessed. What would I do with all the money the world can offer me? At the end of the day all that matters is happiness. That I have in plenty because I have brought happiness into the lives of so many.'

Imagine how much good it would be for the nation if there were more people who thought like Dr Surya.

> We are trustees of knowledge and abilities, to be used for the society at large.

19

The Willow Gladiators

I WAS IN A REMOTE corner of the country, Munnar, when Kapil Dev played one of the greatest games in cricket, scoring 175 runs off 138 balls, against Zimbabwe in the 1983 world cup. He came in to bat when India was at 17/5. India went on to win the world cup for the first time. I heard it on a tiny radio with feeble reception, at 3 in the morning. I thought there would never be another game like Kapil's. Maxwell was not born then.

He lay like a 'dead man' among the ruins. Motionless. His body had given up. He had cramps all over. He could barely breathe. He pleaded with his coach to permit him to retire hurt. He said that he would come back once he was a little better. 'If you go to the dressing room now you will never come back; you won't even be able to walk down the steps back to the ground any more. Your body will crumble like a pack of cards. Get up one last time and do it for your country.' His physio was categorical. He made one last effort to get up; he needed the physio's help to get to his feet; he couldn't get on both feet; he just managed to get one foot on the ground; the other was hanging like a ton of baggage, a most painful attachment to his hip. He wished it wasn't there at all.

Australia still needed another 55 runs to get to the target of 292 set by the Afghanistan cricket team in the league match of the 2023 One Day International (ODI) World Cup, held in India, when the coach coaxed him to stand up.

Glen Maxwell did get up. He looked like a man possessed, a ghost. He knew he couldn't run any more to take the 1s and 2s. He stood there like a motionless rock for the ball to arrive. When it did, nothing moved, except his wrist and hands. It rained down runs from the skies: 6 runs. 4 runs. 6 runs. 4 runs. 4 runs. Then a single to keep the strike. It was the most painful single taken in the history of cricket; his soul moved, but his body wouldn't; he scrambled, dragged his beleaguered body to the other side. It was the biggest manifestation of the human will, generally seen only in battle fields; here bullets were replaced by the lethal cricket ball; bullets kill you in one shot; these white balls torment you every moment. But here, Maxwell was the tormentor and Afghan bowlers the tormented. With 19 deliveries to spare, Australia won by three wickets, with Maxwell on 201 not out, off 128 balls. He hit 21 fours and 10 sixes. It included a reverse sweep 6 off Naveen-ul-Haq. His strike rate was 157.03. Aussie skipper, Pat Cummins, anchored himself at the other end with a 12 off 68 balls. Afghan captain, Rashid Khan, gave Maxwell a bear hug. The hug said it all.

Glen Maxwell played the greatest game ever in the history of cricket, in all formats. He came in to bat when his Australian team were down at 91/7. Everybody expected the team to wind up at 100. Maxwell's 201 propelled the team to the most improbable win in the history of cricket at 293/7. He broke several world records. Maxwells's was the highest score ever made in a One Day International (ODI) run chase. It was the highest score ever made by an Australian in an ODI. It was the 10th highest individual score in ODI history, but possibly the greatest. It was the highest score by a batsman coming in at No 6 or lower. He was the 1st batsman to make an ODI double hundred, not being an opener. It was the 3rd highest individual score in World Cup history.

The world of cricket looked at it with absolute wonder.

India looked completely unbeatable till the final. With 7/57, Mohammed Shami produced the best bowling figures for India in ODIs. Prime Minister Narendra Modi messaged: 'Virat Kohli has exemplified spirit of excellence and perseverance that defines the best of sportsmanship. The bowling by Shami through the World Cup will be cherished for generations to come. Well played, Shami.' Virat Kohli hit his 50th ODI century, making him the player with the greatest number of ODI centuries in international cricket, overtaking Sachin Tendulkar. He is one of the most disciplined sportspersons ever; he never misses a training programme. Just like Dhoni, who is also extremely tough on himself during preparations for matches.

The stories of our cricket heroes are full of trials and tribulations. Indian captain Rohit Sharma grew up in a tiny one-room apartment with his parents and siblings. His father, Gurunath Sharma, was caretaker of the godown of a transport company in Mumbai. Since he was constantly famished, his grandfather took him to his home in Borivali, on the outskirts of Mumbai, to take care of him. This is where he began to play street cricket.

Shami was born to impoverished farmers in Uttar Pradesh. His father, Thausif Ali, encouraged him to play cricket. Mohammed Siraj's father was an autorickshaw driver. His mother worked as a domestic help. He couldn't return home from Australia when his father died due to Covid-19; he went on to take five wickets in the next match a few hours later.

Bumrah, India's strike bowler, and ranked No 1 in the world, said that he struggled hugely after his father's death. For his mother, every day was a fight for survival of the family. He had only one pair of shoes and one T-shirt. He used to wash the T-shirt at night for the next day's use. All these struggles helped him to be mentally and physically tough. Hardik and Kunal Pandya took to cricket when their father was paralysed and bedridden; they played local tournaments to earn their daily bread for the family, because there was nothing else, they knew, that could bring roti and dal on their table. Ravindra Jadeja, considered as the most valuable player in the world, was the son of a watchman in Jamnagar, Gujarat. The stories of the Pathan brothers, Umesh Yadav and Zahir Khan can bring a joyful tear.

The biggest sensation in Indian cricket is twenty-two-year-old Yashasvi Jaiswal, who hit 206 in a test match against England recently. He didn't come from a privileged family. As a teenager, he ran away to Mumbai from Suriyawan, a small town in Uttar Pradesh, as he wanted to play cricket. He had no money. He came from an impoverished family. He slept on Mumbai's footpaths and sold panipuri for a living. He used to jump walls of cricket clubs to watch local players sweat it out. Finally, he was able to pitch a tent on the corner of a cricket ground. He continued to sell panipuri. Suddenly, his saviour descended from nowhere. Jwala Singh, a local cricket coach, came to his roadside panipuri cart one day, late night. Jaiswal told him about his cricketing dreams. He was persistent. To shake him off, Jwala Singh invited him to a batting session. He hit nonstop sixes and Jwala Singh was deeply impressed. He took him under his wing. He took him home, fed him and mentored him. Eventually, Jaiswal became part of India's junior national team and progressed to the senior team through hard work and spectacular performance. He is one of the hottest properties in cricket now.

Possibly the best role model, not just for cricketers alone, has been Rahul Dravid, coach of Indian men's cricket team, who refused to accept a bonus of ₹5 crore, after India won the 2024 T20 World Cup title, arguing that he deserves only as much as the rest of the members of the coaching team. In a world greedy for money, he is such an exception.

I think the biggest hero of the 2023 World Cup, as a team, was Afghanistan. It was Afghanistan's World Cup.

A war-torn country for over three decades, with no cricket stadium of international standards, they stole the hearts of cricket enthusiasts with their incredible game in this World Cup. They beat three former World Cup champions. They almost beat the fourth one as well – Australia. If they beat Australia, they would have certainly made it to the semifinals. Afghan campaign had shades of Morocco at Qatar World Cup Football, 2022. Morocco became the first African and the first Arab team to reach the semifinals of a World Cup.

There are some brilliant women cricketers in India. Smriti Mandhana, Harmanpreet Kaur, Jhulan Goswami and Mitali Raj are exceptionally outstanding. Unfortunately, there are so few patrons for women's cricket worldwide. They are paid poorly, compared to their male counterparts. Commercial endorsements are rare. That is sad. In spite of that, someone like Minnu Mani, a tribal girl from a remote village in Wayanad, has made it into the national team. There is an emerging space for those who are willing to chase their dreams.

Kylian Mbappe, playing with a broken nose and a nose mask in the 2024 Euro Football Championship, is the ultimate symbol of sportsmanship and commitment. He also spoke up against fascist politics, which titled the election against extreme right wing in the Parliament elections in 2024 in France. When he had the power to influence, he spoke up.

> Never give up when the going looks terrible. Energy comes when one is determined not to give up.

20

The Demolition Man

When I got an order from the Ministry of Personnel that I was posted as the commissioner of Delhi Development Authority (DDA), in December 1991, I was completely shocked. I belonged to the Kerala cadre of the IAS and I was working as the director of civil supplies department in Kerala. I had never opted to go on deputation to the government of India. As a matter of convention, only those who opt to go on deputation to the government of India are sent on deputation from the State.

I knew exactly why I was being sent on deputation by the government of Kerala against my wishes: I had written the dissenting note in the palmolein import case, in which the chief minister, minister for food and civil supplies, the chief secretary and six other IAS officers were being prosecuted. All the IAS officers, except the senior most officer in the government hierarchy, were honest people.

We packed our stuff and left for Delhi. It was tough settling down in Delhi. I didn't know any Hindi. I had no friends here. We moved into Asiad Village. The best thing about Asiad Village was that Siri Fort Sports Club was next door. It became so much an integral part of our lives, with both my sons spending a lot of their time there. Eventually, we made lots of good friends in Asiad Village.

My job as land commissioner of the DDA was to acquire the necessary land for development of Delhi. My other crucial duty was to protect DDA land from encroachment.

DDA owned almost 1,00,000 acres of land in Delhi. Nobody in the DDA knew exactly where the land was, how much land was utilised for projects and how much land was encroached upon. There was hardly any scientific inventory of land. We had 36,000 employees in the DDA. What so many people did in the DDA was always a mystery, even to the CEO of the DDA.

In the first week as the commissioner, I told them to prepare a list of all the DDA land and give me a list of encroachments. To my utter shock, I found that over a thousand acres of land was encroached upon. I told them to give me the names of the encroachers, in the order of the extent of land encroached. It was no surprise when I found that the top ten encroachers were politicians. Number one in the list was a former cabinet minister. He was the president of a major political party in Delhi. In 1984, after former prime minister Indira Gandhi's assassination by two Sikh policemen, this mafia leader was mainly instrumental in burning alive over 5000 Sikhs in Delhi. Nothing happened to him or any of the other culprits. Trial is going on against some of these accused, forty years after the holocaust.

When I saw the list of ten encroachers and learnt who they were, I was pretty sure what I was going to do. I called three of my competent officers and told them that the man who was at number one in my list was my first target. They were shocked. They were united in their advice: 'Sir, you don't know Delhi at all. You can't touch him. He is the biggest mafia leader in Delhi, and he is the president of the Party in Delhi. He has burned alive 5000 people and you will be the 5001st.' Behind my back they said: 'This Madrasi can't do anything.' I was reconciled to the fact that all of us south Indians were called 'Madrasis'. I didn't care. I told them: 'I have a simple principle: strike at the biggest criminal first. Since he is number one in the list, he shall be dealt with first.' Guess what was the size of the building built illegally by him? 2,00,000 square feet. It requires audacity to build something like that illegally, so brazenly. He did it because the mafia got away with it in the past. Everybody got away. After all, rules didn't apply to politicians and politically connected mafia. Officers didn't want to pick up unnecessary fights with these people. It was after all very comfortable for officers of the DDA to sit in their air-conditioned officers and affix their signature to notes put up by their subordinates. Why should anyone take on the mafia? It was comfortable for everyone and possibly rewarding for some. See nothing. Hear nothing. Do nothing. You get your salary and all the comforts of being the commissioner of DDA. Once in a while, somebody comes who makes a difference. Subu Rehman, who was the commissioner of DDA till recently, did a lot of innovative work by computerising a lot of data through a software designed by him, called 'idli', making the procedures transparent.

Once I told my trusted three about my plan, we got down to a detailed plan of operation to bring down the building. This is what I do in any project that I undertake: meticulous planning. There were many things to be taken into consideration: the size of the building, the number of bulldozers and other equipment required for bringing it down in the shortest time without causing damage to other properties, the likelihood of political interference, the possibility of physical resistance by the mafia leader and his goons, the number of police force required, etc.

On the D-Day, I gathered all my men and forces in a police station located pretty far away from the site. We never gather our forces in the police station near the site of action because we do not want anyone to know what or where we were going to strike. Only the police commissioner and the DCP of the area were privy to exactly what we were planning to do. In my team, only the three chosen confidants of mine knew where the action was going to happen.

I like to do things in style. I made it dramatic so that the entire power of the state was visible. When we drove into Model Town at 10 a.m., it looked something like a military operation. We had twenty-five massive bulldozers, mounted on large trailers, at the rear. Ahead of that, we had 10,000 policemen in open trucks with guns. In front of that, I was in a Clint Eastwood hat, in an open jeep, along with Spanny, my great Dane. Spanny looked more like a leopard. I had a pistol tucked into my waist. People ran for their lives; they thought that some aliens had invaded the town. They had never seen anything like this. There were hundreds of establishments in the building, including automobile show rooms. I gave them one hour to vacate. Many thought it was an empty threat and didn't move. After an hour, I moved the bulldozers closer. I gave them another hour to vacate. This time, most occupants realised that we were serious. Most moved out. Some didn't. Sharp at noon, the bulldozers got into action. I stood on the road with Spanny for thirty-six hours, till the 2,00,000 square feet had turned into dust. That was my way of repaying for 1984, a small retribution.

Life can be strange: ten days later, the mafia leader walked up to me at a function and hugged me and said: 'You are my friend, as you are the only one who has shown the courage to touch me.'

Next day, it was all over the media: 'The demolition man comes to Delhi.' The name stuck. Over the next five years, we were on the front page of newspapers almost every day. We were lead news on many television channels. We knocked down 14,310 illegal mansions, over the next five years, belonging to the rich and the powerful. I was physically present for all major operations. Most of the work was done by Chawla, Paramjit, Parashar, RR Sharma, Shamim Ahmed and Aftab Iqbal. Not one inch of DDA land was encroached and not one illegal brick was laid in five years. We recovered over 1,200 acres of land, worth a fortune. My boss Mr Jakhanwal, the vice chairman of the DDA, supported me strongly and insulated me from any political interference. He was an honest man. His successor sent me written instructions that demolition can be done only after getting political clearance from the minister. It went where it deserved to go: the waste basket. When the *Times of India* conducted a poll on me, I got 89.6 per cent of Delhiites supporting me. The actual credit goes to my men who showed great courage to take on the mafia.

We never demolished slums, except on three occasions: two were to build roads and the other was from the AIIMS compound. It is easy to demolish slums. But where will the poor people go?

Funny, I never received a telephone call from the powers that be to not demolish any building, even though most of the buildings demolished belonged to the leaders of the ruling party.

I also built. I acquired over 3,750 acres of land to build Dwarka, the biggest sub city built after independence. Still, I don't own a studio apartment anywhere in the world.

> Never be afraid, however powerful your opponent may be.

21

Sherin Shahana: The Wings of Grit

A YOUNG WOMAN FROM Kambalakkad, Wayanad, who has been confined to a wheelchair as a paraplegic since the age of twenty-one, after a fall from the roof, has yet again proven that sheer grit and determination can overcome a physical disability.

When the civil services exam results were declared in 2023, Sherin Shahana secured 913th rank, a feat which she believes has enabled her to feel 'reborn from ashes'.

Shahana's story is not just about the success of a quadriplegic person who defied the odds, but also of a woman who gathered strength after the trauma of a toxic failed marriage. The message embedded in her story is that neither a nightmarish marriage nor brutal torture at the hands of her ex-husband and his family could crush her dreams.

'I am a victim of domestic violence. No. I *was* a victim, not any more. But to realise that I am a survivor, it took me a fall from a twenty-feet-high terrace, followed by around two years of bedridden and depressed life. I have always wanted to be known for my abilities, not my disabilities. Now, I believe that my wish has been fulfilled and if my story would motivate and empower at least one domestic abuse victim, I would be proud,' Shahana told me.

Shahana was born in a poor uneducated Muslim family in Wayanad as the youngest of four daughters of Usman Haji, a daily wage labourer, and Amina, a homemaker.

Two of her sisters had to abandon their studies and get married at an early age. Shahana wanted to study; she was good at it and aimed to get a stable job and provide for her family. She had always dreamed of becoming a civil servant and opted for a bachelor's degree in political science at St Mary's College, Sulthan Bathery.

She has been earning since her college days by taking tuition classes for school students. Soon, she joined master's course in political science in the same college and everything in her life was going smoothly until one day she lost her father to a cardiac arrest. Within a few months, a proposal came from a man. She had to surrender to the family's pressure to get married but on the condition that it should not affect her studies.

Her husband convinced her family that he was a civil engineer and promised her that she could finish her college after marriage. But soon, Shahana realised that her husband did not even go to college and that he was into catering service. She was okay with that; but he and his family did not allow her to continue her studies. Eventually, the abuse and violence began.

'He beat me up almost every day. As I was not allowed to go to college, I borrowed notes from my friends and studied. He punished me by running a razor blade all over my body and making me stand under the shower for hours when I was bleeding all over. I could do nothing but cry. If my father were there, I could have told him. But I did not want my mother, who was highly diabetic, to know about my plight. One day, she noticed the scars and found the truth. I was brought back to my house. The local mosque committee convinced me to go back once again; after the torture became intolerable, I left that house,' Shahana said.

The fall that changed Shahana's life happened on 31 May 2017, nearly five months after she left her husband's house. It was the last day of her MA final semester examination.

She returned home after the examination and, as it was about to rain, she went to the terrace to collect the clothes which were hung there to dry. Accidentally, she slipped and fell from the terrace. 'When the doctors said that I would have to be fully bedridden for at least one and a half years, I was shocked. But I was happy, too, as I would not have to go back to my husband's house. As expected, neither my husband nor his family came to see me or enquire about me. My disability was an excuse for him to divorce me. He has remarried and has two kids now,' Shahana said.

'I was so depressed and wished to end my life, but my physical disability failed me. I put a noose around my neck and tied it to the window bar and then tried to slip off the wheelchair. But it failed. I tried to cut my vein but failed again as I could not even hold a piece of the blade with my non-functional finger. One day, my mother found me trying to cut my vein and she could not do anything but cry pathetically. But later, she said, "If Allah has put you in this condition, he surely is keeping something good for you."'

'Now, I understand what she meant,' Shahana said.

Eventually, Shahana accepted the reality and tried to regain her health. Continuous physiotherapy started restoring movement in her hands. She began reading books and using the phone and became active on social media. Gradually, she started performing her daily routine independently. She even started using a pen and pencil on her own. Once she received a motorised wheelchair, her movements, too, became easier, and she started going out.

'I made a lot of friends online and one of them was Muralee Thummarukudy, the operations manager at the crisis management branch of the UN Environment Programme. He is like a father to me. He has mentored, encouraged and guided me. Later, I started tuition classes for school kids, and it encouraged me to get back to my studies. My mother and sisters were my pillars of support,' Shahana said.

Thummarukudy said that Shahana's willpower and determination inspired him. 'I first met her when she sought my help with a wheelchair. Eventually, we became so connected. Sherin's life is a true motivation to all of us,' he said.

In 2019, after she cleared the national eligibility test, Dr Jobin S. Kottaram, a motivational speaker who runs Absolute IAS Academy, approached Shahana, inviting her to his special batch 'Chithrasalabham' (Butterflies), which trains differently abled persons for the civil services exam.

'Jobin sir encouraged me to dust up my UPSC dreams. He trained me and guided me. I could not clear it in the first attempt, but he motivated me to try again,' Shahana said. Kottaram said that Shahana had to work more than any other candidate in the exam. 'She made use of digital tools to overcome her limitations. It is a proud moment for all of us,' he said.

Even after getting into the civil service, the government would not give her a posting, citing her disabilities. Rishiraj took up her case with the cabinet secretary. Former cabinet secretary K.M. Chandrasekhar used his connections to put her in touch with the right people. I spoke to the secretary, Department of Personnel. The cabinet secretary and the secretary, DOPT, were empathetic and allotted her to the Railway Management Service.

Sherin Shahana is an inspiration for everyone.

You can overcome any limitation.

22

You Are a Unique Creation

'THE WORLD IS FULL of people trying to tidy us up, straighten us out, round us off, smooth us down. You will be told to "shape up or ship out",' says Richard Craze in his book *The 7 Bad Habits of Highly Ineffective People*.[1]

The entire world is conniving to convince each of us that we are just a drop in the ocean, that we are nobodies. We are told to fall in line. When we believe we are nobodies, it is easy for the system to control us. It is easy for parents at home. They don't have to sit with each kid to know their feelings and emotions.

It is easy for the teachers in school. Imagine if the teacher had to rack her brains to unravel the mystery of fifty kids who are wired differently. Now if they all have the same circuit and the same fuse, thank God, it becomes easy. They don't ask unnecessary questions or show unnecessary emotions. No messing around what is right and what is wrong. Why waste time on debating, when the teacher knows it all. It is so easy for the pujari, the imam and the pastor. No unnecessary questions about your God. It is so easy to govern when everyone believes in the same thing.

The fact is each one of us is designed and destined to be different. You are a unique creation. Nobody like you has ever existed on the planet, nobody like you is alive anywhere on the face of the earth today and nobody like you will ever be born.

Nobody is created dumb. I believed I was dumb until I told myself that I was not. I strongly began to believe that I was unique in every way. I decided that I did not want to be like anybody else. If we have the guts to believe, each of us is a potential genius. You have incredible talents. Your children have incredible talents. Most of the parents believe that their children are born with X amount of intelligence and talent and nothing more. We hear so often in schools and families: 'Look at her, she is such a genius,' or 'He is so talented,' or 'You are good for nothing.'

Every child has the potential to be a genius. If you believe in yourself, sky is not the limit. You can do and be everything you dream of. Teachers need to understand that their words carry weight. They can have a lasting effect on the students. If a teacher calls a student a 'moron' or dismisses the student's potential, chances are that the student would be deeply affected, with lasting consequences.

Parents need to sit down with their kids every day and tell them how different they are from all other kids. There is so much peer pressure on kids to be like their friends. It is tough to be the odd one out. We have to tell our kids that it is okay to stand out. Children, tell your parents that you don't want to be like others.

I had this interesting man for my neighbour in Asiad Village in Delhi for almost eight years, when I was the commissioner of DDA. He lived in a single room apartment. In his mid-sixties, he still had his own brand of hippie hair. He ate very little, thought a lot and used to play the veena in his spare time. On his regular walk in the Siri Fort Sport Club, we would come across each other often and he would ask me: 'Alphons, what about your dreams?' I told him how disappointed I was about the fact that India was going nowhere, while the whole world was marching along so fast on the path of progress. He would tell me: 'Alphons, we still have hope; all that we need is to allow our children to dream for themselves.'

When the world slept, my neighbour in the Asiad Village designed missiles and the A-bomb for the country. His life was always centred around dreams. You guessed it right: I am talking about Dr A.P.J. Abdul Kalam. He moved on from the tiny one bedroom in Asiad Village into the 250-bedroom Rashtrapati Bhavan in 2003, when he became the president of India. What a unique man, with a unique dream! He was a dreamer and got the nation to dream big.

If you are unique, you must have a unique dream, not your parent's or teacher's. What is a unique dream? It is about your way of making the world happier. A dream is not about just yourself; it is about yourself in the society. By this, I do not mean that you shouldn't care about your life. If you don't care about yourself, who will? However, you could include the 'other' bit in your life. There is no way that my family and I are going to survive happily on this planet while the rest of the world is miserable.

I have decided that I am unique. Whenever I get into trouble because of my outspokenness, my wife would ask me: 'Why can't you be like them?' I would tell her: 'I can't be like any of them because I am created the way I am; I am unique.'

Some of the most loved and respected people in the world are possibly not the most 'beautiful' people by societal definition. You just need to look at the mirror and say to yourself: 'Wow, I am great.' You don't need to take endless selfies every ten minutes, post them on Instagram and WhatsApp and wait for 'likes'. It destroys you when your friends get a 1000 likes and you get a few less. Why do you need anybody's 'likes'? To hell with them. Love yourself. Others will automatically love you. Beauty salons try to convert you into the image of the movie goddess. Why do you want to look like a movie goddess? Because you are uncomfortable being you. Most people want to look like anyone but themselves. The first law of happiness is be happy the way you are created. I was not the best-looking guy in the IAS academy. But one thing I know for sure was that I was deeply loved by my batchmates and later by the citizen. That relationship continues. Its ok if some don't love me.

One has to be unique in one's thoughts, emotions and actions. One needs to make unique contributions.

> You are unique. Nobody like you has ever been created in the history of the universe. Love yourself. Have your unique dreams. Chase them to the end and you will get there.

23

Listen to the Sound of Silence

A WISE OLD KING in India, when he grew old, called his only son and told him: 'I want you to take over as the king as early as possible. Of course, you have to learn a lot before you can take over. Go out and learn everything that you ought to know.'

The prince went around the kingdom. He travelled extensively and learnt all about administration and justice. He came back after six months and told the king: 'I am ready to be the king.' The king asked him: 'Son, what have you learnt?' The prince told him: 'I have learnt all about administration. I know how the army wins a war. I know how the public offices work. I know how the justice system works. I have learnt all about the subjects of the kingdom.' The king told him: 'Son, you are not yet ready to be the king; go out in the nature, learn all about the countryside, learn about forests and wildlife; learn about the universe.'

The prince left for the forests. He travelled extensively and returned after a year. He told the king: 'I have learnt all about nature. I have learnt the names of the trees and every creature which lives in the forest; I have heard the roar of the lion and sound of the wind. I have learnt how we can co-exist. I am ready to be the king.'

The king told him: 'Son, you are not ready to be the king yet. There is still a lot more to learn. Go back to the forest.' The prince left again. He spent a long time in the forest. He came back and told his father: 'Father, I am now ready to be the king. I have heard the thunderous sound of the sun breaking out in the morning. I heard the sound of honey forming in the belly of the flower. I heard the sound of silence.'

The king told him: 'Son, you are ready to be the king. You have heard what nobody else can hear; you have heard the sound of silence.'

The prince took over as the king. He became one of the greatest kings of all time.

Happiness is our ability to hear the sound of silence. It is our ability to enjoy solitude. The 'sound of silence' is nothing but the ability to hear one's own thoughts and the heartbeat of the world.

Most achievers in the history of the world have spent time listening to the sound of silence. Ram spent fourteen long years in exile. He was not sleeping. He was listening intensely to his inner self. He was listening to the whispers of the universe, which came coded with loud messages. Jesus Christ spent forty days contemplating on the mountains before he began his public life. Every day, during his active public life, he retreated to the forests to be with himself and his inner voice.

Long before the world thought about metaphysics, India had a vibrant philosophical and theological milieu. Buddha, deeply troubled by the cruelty inflicted by humans on each other, sat under a tree and achieved enlightenment. That led to the path of realisation for the world. The long conversation between Krishna and Arjuna on the battlefield, on good and evil and one's duties, as detailed in the Bhagavad Gita, originated in the inner core of Krishna in contemplation. Prophet Muhammad spent time meditating in a cave in Mount Hira. Sufism took its root from deep introspection and the urge to connect to the sublime in one's own way. The world changed from what they discovered in their silence. If only we lived true to their teachings and our inner voice!

Every day before I go to sleep, I do two things: I listen to music and spend time in silence. I don't call it meditation. It is fundamentally looking at whether one is falling in place in the scheme of the universe. Unless one is falling in place with the scheme of the universe, one's life is useless, because we are here to make the world a little better with our lives. There are a million ways to do it.

Therefore, looking back at the end of the day and listening to the voices of people, whose life one was expected to enrich that day, makes sense. Their inner voices talk to us if we care to listen. That gives us the resolve to make our tomorrows better. Each day calls for course correction. Each day is also a day for celebration, as we would have touched some lives positively in some ways. It is important to celebrate our small victories.

The loudest voices come to us in solitude.

Enjoy solitude. Listen to your inner self; set apart time every day.

24

Sonam Wangchuk: The Snow Man

THE MOVIE *3 IDIOTS* was a blockbuster. The character Phunsukh Wangdu, one of the three 'idiots', was based on Sonam Wangchuk. This 'idiot' went on to win global recognition for what he has done in real life: Magsaysay Award in 2018, Rolex Award for Enterprise in 2016, Global Award for Sustainable Architecture in 2017, Real Heroes Award in 2008, Ashoka Fellowship for Social Entrepreneurship in 2002, the UNESCO Chair for Earth Architecture for India in 2014, Green Teacher Award by *Sanctuary Asia* Magazine in 2005 and many more.

I attended his interaction at India International Centre, Delhi, in 2023. The audience was deeply impressed.

Sonam Wangchuk was born in 1966 in Alchi, Leh. His father was a politician. Since there were no schools near his village, he was taught by his mother at home till he was nine, in his mother tongue. His father then took him to a school in Srinagar, where he was enrolled in a formal school. He did not comprehend a word of what his teachers or classmates spoke. His classmates thought that he was stupid. At the age of eleven, he escaped to Delhi all alone, went to the principal of Vishesh Kendriya Vidyalaya and managed to get himself an admission in the school. After completing school, he enrolled in the National Institute of Technology (NIT), Srinagar, in Mechanical Engineering.

After graduating from NIT in 1988 he, along with five other friends, started Students' Educational and Cultural

Movement of Ladakh (SECMOL), whose objective was to bring about reforms in the government school system in Ladakh. He was extremely critical of the way government schools were run. He felt that they were teaching nothing of relevance. At the same time, he believed that the government school system should be reformed, as this is where ordinary citizens sent their children.

In 1994, he launched Operation New Hope. It was a triangular collaboration of the civil society, the village community and the government. Village education committees were formed to take ownership of government schools; teachers were trained in student-friendly methodologies. They also started rewriting school textbooks and publishing them. The results were dramatic: the pass percentage went up from 5 per cent to 55 per cent in seven years.

He founded the SECMOL Alternative Campus, where the admission criterion was failure – only those who failed in the examination could get admission here. This is possibly the only school in the world where the admission criterion is FAILURE, in capital letters.

The foundation year at SECMOL is a year-long residential programme for forty students. Preference is given to students from disadvantaged backgrounds and from regions, religions and ethnicities generally not represented in the mainstream. Schedule is packed from early morning till night. The medium of instruction is Ladakhi. They are taught basic English conversation, science with focus on solar energy, nature, health and environmental studies. They are also assigned the responsibility of running the campus, from cleaning toilets to shopping, cooking, gardening and dairying. Morning lectures involve current issues and self-development. Evenings are filled with co-curricular activities: debates, quiz, dancing, games, movies, etc. They are also taught Ladakhi history and geography, Ladakhi language and literature, computers, basic maths and basic health. They also learn ice skating and how to run a marathon.

SECMOL also runs short-term courses of ten to fourteen days. In December and January, they run annual camps for rural youth who have just done their class 10 examinations. The main objective of the camp is to build self-confidence in children. They learn English, how to generate solar energy and all about collective survival of the planet. They are also taught Ladakhi history and geography along with Ladakhi songs and dance.

SECMOL also organises 'The Sun and Earth Natural Building Festival'. Participants are taught the essentials of mud and solar construction. World leaders with hands-on experience teach children.

SECMOL tries to produce enough food for their consumption. But because of the vagaries of nature, it is not sufficient. They have come up with procedures to preserve vegetables since almost nothing grows in winter. Whatever is additionally required is bought from farmers in the neighbourhood.

The SECMOL campus, initially completely barren, is now a thriving greenery. They do not use chemical fertilizers at all. They use cow dung for manure. Kitchen waste is eaten by the cows.

With the supportive and creative system SECMOL created, children went on to excel in their chosen fields. They became acclaimed teachers, politicians, filmmakers, authors and entrepreneurs. They learnt about ways where planet Earth and humankind could exist together for a long time.

Sonam and the students together designed low-cost solar-heated buildings, made of earth. The buildings in the campus are heated without burning electric heaters or fuels such as firewood or gas. The passive solar design absorbs heat from the sun and stores it. The main features that keep the buildings warm are insulation in the roof, outer walls and under the floor; thick earthen walls and floors; greenhouses attached to the south side for winter; greenhouses removed in springtime to prevent overheating; skylights covered with glass to keep warm air indoors; natural lighting to save on electricity consumption; and south-facing windows to absorb light.

In winter, huge plastic sheets are rolled down from the roof to make a greenhouse which works as a power collector. In summer, it is rolled up to prevent overheating. Some buildings are made of straw–clay bricks. The buildings at Phey campus are rammed earth. The wood waste generated during construction is stuffed into the ceiling to prevent heat loss through the roof. The outer walls are insulated by a jacket wall. The 6-inch gap between the two walls is filled with saw dust and wood shavings. Sometimes, cow dung is also used as insulation.

SECMOL campus is mostly solar-powered. Solar energy is used for pumping, lighting and heating. Solar water heaters and solar cookers are used. Drinking water is pumped up from a borewell using solar power.

In 2015 Sonam established the Himalayan Institute of Alternatives (HIAL) in Phyang, Ladakh, so that young people could study and find indigenous solutions to the problems of their own environment.

Sonam talks about the philosophy of HIAL: 'Everything around us has changed drastically in the last 150 years: from riding on horseback to flying by aeroplanes, from using pigeons to mail and emails and smartphones; but in our schools, colleges and classrooms almost nothing has changed. Chalk, talk and paper knowledge, paper degrees and paper examinations – all too papery, outdated and theoretical and very little that prepares us for the real world happens here. No wonder graduates coming out of most of our colleges and universities finish a ritual and get their degrees but are highly unemployable, according to various studies. Very often, employers end up re-educating the fresh recruits at their own expense. HIAL is a collaborative exercise between learners and facilitators. It aims to inspire the seekers of knowledge to explore both outside and within themselves. Instead of solving problems with conventional 3Rs, we encourage learners to solve problems using 3Hs: Bright Head, Kind Heart and Skilled Hands.'[1]

Some of the courses offered at HIAL are: Food processing, Responsible tourism, Eco-Responsive building, Ecology and Ice Stupa, and HIAL Experimental Leadership Module.

In 2016, Sonam won the Rolex Award for innovation for conceptualising and executing ice stupas. Water flows down in abundance in winter in the Himalayas. When spring comes, all the water has flown down to the valley and there is acute shortage of water for drinking and agriculture. The idea was simple: water maintains its level.

Pipes were laid from a reservoir a few hundred metres upstream. Sonam mounted the exit of these pipes a few hundred metres from the ground. As the water fell from that height, in the winter months in Ladakh, with a temperature of -30°C to -50°C outside, the water would freeze before it hit the ground and slowly a huge ice stupa, roughly 30–50 metres high, would form. He let the piped water first freeze at the ground level and then mounted more and more pipes as the thickness of the ice grew. So the cost was minimal. He built these ice stupas right next to the villages so that people didn't have to travel far. When spring came, these ice stupas melted slowly, providing enough water to the villagers. Since these ice cones extend vertically upwards towards the sun, it receives very little sunshine and therefore melts very slowly, releasing only the quantity of water required by a village. The first one was built at Phey village. Then it was replicated all over. Agriculture has become viable in hundreds of villages, and the mountains which were deserted have become lush green.

Sonam Wangchuk says about his life belief: 'Every drop in the ocean counts. I request each and every individual to be part of this wonderful movement and show how the power of individual action can achieve a green planet.'[2]

On 6 March 2024, he launched 'Climate Fast for 21 days' to draw the attention of the country towards issues he felt were crucial for Ladakh.

> Traditional knowledge and wisdom are critical in solving local problems.
>
> Innovative education and action are the key to the future of the world.

25

Vasudhaiva Kutumbakam

IN 2007, SHEELA WAS driving home from shopping in Cochin. As it was raining, the traffic was moving at a snail's pace. She heard a scream from the bushes on the side of the road. She parked her car on the roadside and the shrill scream grew louder. She waded through the puddle and the overgrowth of vegetation, and there was the source of the painful scream. She went closer. It looked like a dog. It was lying in a puddle of filthy water. She returned to the car, took her drinking water and a paper carton that was lying in the boot. She poured water over the bundle of flesh and got rid of the mud and the filth. The little dog had no hair or skin. Its eyes were popping out. Sheela couldn't let it die like that. She dragged it into the paper carton and managed to get it into the boot. It was light: maybe a maximum of 5 kg.

She took her to the government veterinary hospital, near the district collector's residence. This is where she used to treat all her pet dogs. The vets here were great. They had one look at the bundle of flesh and said that she was beyond treatable. They advised her to take her to a private veterinary hospital in the city. At the private hospital, the doctors said that there was not much hope of saving her, as she was badly burned. Sheela insisted. The doctors said that they could give it a try, but she would have to be in the ICU for a long time, and it would cost a lot of money. Sheela told them that it didn't matter how much it costs, she must be saved. Thus began the long ordeal. She was in the ICU for a month, after which she was transferred to the general ward. She could leave the hospital only after three months. They couldn't do anything about her eyes. She would be blind.

The doctors explained what may have happened to the dog: 'It is a Pomeranian. You don't see stray Pomeranians on the street. It must have been somebody's pet. They must have thrown it out when they moved home. It is about three years old.' My wife asked: 'How come she was burnt all over?' The doctor replied: 'It must have been wandering around and must have walked into somebody's house or shop when it was hungry and they may have poured hot water on the poor thing. I don't see how it was burnt all over, otherwise.' What kind of people could have done this to this innocent little creature?

I didn't know anything about these happenings till I came home one day and saw a Pomeranian on the veranda of my house in Kadavanthara, Cochin. Those days, I was the MLA from Kanjirappally and I would come home only once in ten days from my constituency. As my car entered the driveway, this little stranger barked furiously. My wife came out with a prompt explanation: 'It is a stray dog. It is blind. It was in the hospital. Somebody is coming from Bangalore within a week to adopt her. Let her be on the veranda till they come.' I consented, even though I was not sure how our other pets would take it. We already had three dogs and two cats. After three days, Sheela told me: 'It's raining and a strong wind is blowing and its uncomfortable for her on the veranda. Shall I let her into the house? It will be for just a few days.' I agreed. I also enquired about the arrival of the good soul from Bangalore who was supposed to adopt her. She said that they will come 'shortly'. The 'shortly' never happened. From day one, I knew that she was here for good. So we decided to give her a name: Silky. To our great surprise, we found that our other pets were more than accommodating to

Silky. She became the centre of attention. Since she needed a bit of extra care, we let her sleep in our bedroom.

Unfortunately, Bubbly, our labrador, died of a liver collapse in 2010. We wept. She was the most affectionate one. One of our cats, too, died prematurely. These were trying times for us.

When we shifted to Delhi in 2011, we had the remaining four of them sent to Delhi by train. Anmol, our man Friday from DDA days, came down to take them in the train. We settled down in Noida, on the outskirts of Delhi.

This is when Sheela started feeding street dogs. We call them 'community dogs'. Every day, she would make a bucket biryani and go around all the streets of sector 15, Noida, and feed them. Sometimes she had to face hostile residents, who threatened to manhandle her. They said she had no business feeding street dogs. Twice she had to call the police. Ever since, she would keep with her a Delhi High Court order which permitted feeding of community dogs. We found a fantastic vet, Dr Samad Jain, in Vasundhara. I have never come across a vet who loves animals so much.

Sheela adopted three more cats from the street while in Noida: Chu, Peeli and Nuzi. Unfortunately, two of them passed away prematurely. Two of our dogs, Crisle and Bully, also passed away due to old age. Those were traumatic experiences. I can't really explain in words how it feels when our pets die. It was so much like our dearest family members dying. We wept for days.

When we moved to Delhi after I was made the union minister for tourism, we took our pets to Lodhi Estate. Sheela also adopted six community dogs from Noida. So we had seven dogs and two cats at our new residence. The front lawn was for cats and the back lawn was for the dogs. They all lived happily. Silky continued to sleep in our bedroom. When I got back home every day, she would sit with me on the sofa with her head on my lap. When she died of old age in 2021, we were unconsolable. She brought so much happiness into our lives. Every pet does. Only those who have pets will know the immense joy they bring to their lives. They demand so little and give so much.

When I completed my tenure in Parliament, we moved to a first-floor apartment in North Avenue, where we couldn't keep our dogs. We hired a ground floor apartment for the dogs. Sheela feeds all the community dogs in North Avenue. She also takes any sick dog to the veterinary hospital. The local NDMC doctor, Dr Sanjay Kumar, has been very helpful. She has also started feeding monkeys fruits, as North Avenue has hundreds of them. They come to the kitchen window in the morning for their morning snacks. Then she goes to the neighbourhood park with fruits. None has ever attacked her.

I know so many people across the country who do such things for animals. What Sheela does is possibly just a drop in the ocean. But is certainly matters and makes many animals happy.

Last year, I impleaded in person in a case before the Supreme Court of India regarding eliminating stray dogs.[1] There is a massive battle in the Supreme Court and outside on the issue. There are a lot of people who feel that all community dogs (they call them 'stray troubles') must be eliminated. What I have suggested in my impleading petition is simple: India's philosophy is 'vasudhaiva kutumbakam', which means that the universe is one. We all need to co-exist. The survival of the planet depends on co-existence. Animal Birth Control (ABC) programmes must be implemented effectively, so that in the long run there will be no community dogs on the streets. Meanwhile, let us keep our community dogs happy.

Happy dogs don't bite. Only hungry dogs do. Keep some food outside your gate in a little pot for these dogs. Keep a little water as well.

Man–animal conflict has been on for a long time, ever since man encroached on their domain. Millions of acres of their habitat have been burnt down for human habitation. Wildlife moves out of the forest to human habitat in search of food, as the forest does not have enough food for them. The solution is not to sedate, transport and dump them in a neighbouring state. We need to find lasting solutions. I hope that the Supreme Court disposes off the petition in the spirit of 'vasudhaiva kutumbakam'.

Let us all learn to survive together. Humans have no monopoly over the resources of the planet. We need to learn to share.

> Everything in this universe is part of us. Let us be kind to animals. Let us do our bit to make them happy. They in turn will give us great happiness.

26

P.U. Thomas: The Peon Who Feeds 7,500 People a Day

P.U. THOMAS WAS A peon in the operation theatre of Kottayam Medical College. For the past thirty years, he has been providing free breakfast, lunch and dinner to 7,500 persons every day.

I have known P.U. Thomas since 1988, when I was the district collector of Kottayam. I was the Ex-officio Chairman of Kottayam Medical College Governing Body for about three and a half years. I got to know him then and I have kept in touch with him ever since.

Who is this peon who inspires millions?

His journey is amazing and inspiring. He is the founder and leading guide of Navajeevan Trust. P.U. Thomas is popularly known as Thomas chettan (elder brother Thomas). He is a legend. He is a unique example of how an ordinary person, a class four government employee, can render extraordinary service to the poor and needy. His presence, words and care heal hundreds of suffering people.

P.U. Thomas comes from an agricultural family in Athirampuzha village, near Kottayam. Hailing from a poverty-ridden family, Thomas was unable to continue his school education beyond class 7. In 1976, at the age of seventeen, Thomas suffered a severe ulcer in his stomach due to lack of food. The doctor in the district hospital advised urgent surgery. He was admitted to the hospital and had to spend sixteen days there for the surgery. He decided that after recovery, he would come back to the hospital with food. The surgery was done and Thomas recovered.

After his discharge from the hospital, he would visit patients at the medical college every day, carrying boiled rice and curry packed in banana leaves. In 1969, after the hospital management noticed his sincerity, commitment and service to the downtrodden, he was given a temporary job in the medical college at Kottayam as a gardener. In 1980, he got a permanent job as a peon in the psychiatry ward. He continued to provide food for the poor.

It was at this juncture that Thomas took the initiative to start a shelter for those suffering from mental health issues, in a single room establishment in a lodge, in 1988. This is how Navajeevan Trust was born. Navajeevan has rehabilitated more than 4,000 homeless people, with mental problems, so far. Today, Navajeevan Trust is working out of a multi-story building with 156 inmates. Navajeevan Trust is spread across 5 acres of land in Villooni, a rural area in Arpookara gram panchayat, 4 kilometres from the Kottayam medical college. A 3-storied building was constructed with the help of voluntary organisations. The building has 22 rooms, apart from rooms for prayer, library, recreation, storage and dining. Financial assistance from religious, government, foreign agencies is neither sought nor received. Thomas fears that such help would curtail the freedom of action and efficiency of the administration of the institution.

Majority of the beneficiaries of Navajeevan are homeless, destitute psychiatric patients. They are from all parts of the country, speak different languages and belong to different religions and cultures. Navajeevan campus has no armed guards or security. There are no isolation cells for the patients. So far, nearly 3,500 patients have been treated and sent back to their families. But there are instances where their own families have rejected them, upon which they become inmates and members of Navajeevan. Numerous women have become permanent residents of Navajeevan and are working as volunteers. There are elderly people, who are thrown out from home, by the cruelty of their close relatives. Currently, around fifty inmates are elderly people, mostly bedridden, requiring palliative care. There are families, who cannot look after their bedridden parents or elders due to utter poverty. Navajeevan, if convinced, takes them for rehabilitation free of cost.

At present, Navajeevan is distributing hygienic and delicious food to nearly 7,500 patients daily, in seven hospitals in Kottayam. The food is cooked at the central kitchen, located at the Trust campus and ferried to the hospitals. Thomas oversees the entire process. It happens with incredible precision.

In the nearby hospitals, Navajeevan volunteers are always available, especially in casualty wards, when emergency cases arrive. Patients from various places come to Navajeevan Trust for aid. They are provided with medicines collected as donations from medical stores. Navajeevan provides assistance for diagnostic investigations. They also distribute clothes when required. Navajeevan's ambulance provides free transportation. Blood donation is also provided for poor patients.

Thomas is invited to colleges and schools across Kerala, for their orientation programmes. His life itself is a message for the younger generations. Navajeevan also makes earnest efforts to make government hospitals at Kottayam a better place. The medical college owns a beautiful garden and a green campus, through the efforts of the 'Clean and Green' initiative of Navajeevan. He also distributes tree saplings to visitors of the trust. The cleaning of toilets, wards, canals and drainages in the hospital premises are being done by Navajeevan.

Navajeevan Trust does lots of other things: It provides free dialysis, builds houses for the poor, promotes cultivation of organic vegetables, runs anti-drug campaigns and promotes reading habit.

P.U. Thomas, at seventy-five, has a busy schedule. He wakes up at 4.30 a.m. and, after prayer, goes straight to Navajeevan. The residents earnestly await their 'Papa'. He supervises the preparation of breakfast and then meets bedridden patients, checking on their health conditions. Then he oversees the dispatch of food to hospitals. After breakfast with the inmates, whom he affectionately calls 'makkal' (children), he proceeds to the hospitals. There, he listens to patients and their bystanders in dire need of support, financial or otherwise. Having worked as a supporting staff in Kottayam Medical College for nearly five decades, he has a long association with the hospital and has access to doctors and nursing staff in all departments. His gentleness and spirit of service has earned him their love and respect.

> You don't need to have a 'big job' or have a lot of money to make a difference. It's all in your heart.

27

Live Happy

LIFE IS A LONG journey to find an answer to the question 'why was I born?' To me, the only answer to the above question is: 'To be happy and to make others happy.' The others include not only human beings but also everything that is animate and inanimate.

How do we make something that is inanimate happy? By the simple act of not wrecking it. We make the air happy by not polluting it. We make the river happy by letting it be.

But what makes you happy? Is it lots of money? Is it lots of material things money can buy? Is it a handsome boyfriend? A pretty girlfriend? What is 'handsome' and 'pretty' anyway? Who has given anybody the right to define them? Is it a million 'likes' on Instagram and Facebook? What about the gaping emptiness in your heart when you have all of these in good measure?

I am not for a moment saying that wanting material things or making money is bad. Make money. Make plenty. Live it up. But again, what is 'live it up'? Can we just live for the moment all our lives? It has to be part of a larger scheme of things. The basic fact is happiness does not come from outside; it comes from within you. Happiness comes from the feeling that one is on the path to fulfilment. Happiness comes from the feeling that we have made a difference to the world around us, that we have brought a smile to somebody's face.

You can only be truly happy when you know where you want to go and you know you are well on the path towards it. It is like being a mountaineer. They know their destination. As they take the little steps towards the peak, they sit back occasionally and take stock. 'Are we on the right track?' They might fall and break their bones. Even in their pain and grief, they are still happy because they still have sight of where they want to go. But we don't need to behave like mountaineers all the time. Occasionally, one needs to take a 'walk to nowhere', with no particular destination, just breathing the fresh air, imbibing the scent of the soil and the fragrance of unknown trees and flowers. You need to let your hair down and dance to fill your soul. It can't be business all the time.

Sherpa Nongi wanted to be on top of Mount Everest. From the time he was a kid, he was sure he wanted to be up there. One day, while returning from a mountaineering class on a weekend, he was run over by a bus, and he lost his right leg, from the knee down. In the hospital, he still talked about being on top of the Everest. His mother told him: 'Son, I would be so glad if you are ever able to walk normally again.' But Nongi told her: 'Mama, I will climb the Everest.' This was in 2000. In 2004, he was on top of the Everest, with one leg; the other was an artificial leg.

Happiness is when you reach where you want. But happiness is also on the route of the journey. In fact, the journey is more important than the final arrival. My batchmates, Ravinder Singh (we call him Chiefy) and Dilip Heble, go trekking in the Himalayas often. I asked both of them to talk to me about the experience. They declined: 'We can't explain in words; it is a sublime feeling.'

We go step by step. Every achievement breeds in us the craving for bigger achievements, which requires greater effort and bigger energy. That is how I taught myself in college. I failed miserably so often. I was the butt of jokes. But I hung in there.

There is another danger: far too many people are too happy too easily. IAS officers feel fulfilled the moment they cross the gates of Mussoorie academy. A politician becomes far too happy when he becomes a minister. A doctor is happy the moment he becomes a consultant with a seven-figure retainer. A teacher becomes overjoyed when she becomes a principal. A businessman is happy the moment he has a bungalow and a Mercedes in his garage. They are happy becoming what their parents and the society expected them to be. To possess is in our DNA.

Some nations believe that the most important mission in a nation's life is to grow and grow. But for a select few, like Bhutan, the most important objective is happiness: how happy are the people at large? Bhutan has a tiny GDP; its per capita income in 2024 is about $3200. But the people of this tiny nation, living on top of the Himalayas, in adverse geographical conditions, are much happier than people living in countries ten times its per capita income.

When I was finalising this book, the list of happiest nations in the world in 2024 was published. Tiny Finland is at the top.

Happiness is in simple things and most of them come free. Just get out of your shell, and it is all out there.

I am not a saint or a hermit. I have no intention of being one either. I live it up. But I possess little and I am very happy. I have only one blue jacket. It is forty-five years old. I bought it in Delhi in 1979, on my way to the IAS Academy in Mussoorie, as an IAS probationer. Why do I need a second jacket when the one I have is good. Most of my black trousers are at least twenty years old and have turned to shades of grey. Still, I used to be one of the most elegantly dressed MPs. I never have a meal or a coffee in any upmarket coffee shop or restaurant. The price of the coffee is enough to teach a child for a month.

As the commissioner of DDA, I acquired 3,750 acres of land to build Dwarka, the biggest sub city built in India after independence. But I do not possess even a studio apartment anywhere in the world. After my mother passed away of Covid-19, we gave away five million meals. It was greatly fulfilling. Money has such uses. Maybe it all sounds stupid. But I am happy being stupid.

We will never be happy at the end of the day if the rest of the world is miserable and some of us are rocking. Warren Buffet is giving away 99 per cent of his wealth in philanthropy. It is known that Bill Gates is keeping less than 5 per cent of his wealth for his family. In India, Shiv Nadar gave away over ₹1,300 crore in 2023. Nandan Nilekani, Sudha Narayanamurthy, Shibulal and Kris Gopalakrishnan of Infosys and Asim Premji of Wipro donate considerable amount of wealth. One Ajit Issac from Bangalore, about whom I had never heard of, gave away ₹115 crore last year. Ratan Tata built a state-of-the-art pet hospital at Mumbai for ₹165 crore. But the philanthropic instinct of Indians is pretty pathetic. Less than 2 per cent of people give money to charity.

There are so many ways to give. It need not necessarily be in money. Those who have money can make a bit of an effort to spend a little less on non-essentials and give the money saved to a good cause. There are so many institutions out there doing a great job, starved of resources. You could even begin at home by paying for your domestic helpers, children's education, so that the next generation do not have to live a miserable life. There is no harm in cooking a little extra food so that the children of domestic helps get a nutritious meal once in a while. Those who do not have money to give away could volunteer time to work for a cause. There are so many institutions in your neighbourhood who would be happy if you give them a few hours of yours in a week. You could plant trees and nurture them for a while until they can grow independently.

> Happiness should be our ultimate goal, not material objects. Happiness not just for oneself but for as many as possible.

28

The Everywhere Man

THE STORY GOES OF a class teacher who gave an exercise to the students to write what they want to become in life. Most of them wrote a profession they wanted to take up, such as, 'I want to be a doctor' or 'I want to be a teacher'. One student was very different in his answer. He wrote, 'I want to become happy.' Seeing the answer, the teacher told the student, 'I think you did not understand the question.' The student replied, 'I think you did not understand life.'

That kid is my youngest brother, George. He is the eighth in my family of eleven children. He is a phenomenon.

Recently in his TEDx talk, George talked about a huge chunk of our eight billion humanity globally, who are uncared and often unwanted, whom he calls the 'people in to the peripheries' of the society. To bring meaning to their lives, George chose to become a Catholic priest. He belongs to the Claretian congregation and lives in Bangalore. His congregation is guided by one dictum: do what is timely, urgent and effective. For him, to bring joy to human lives is the mission.

What did George do with his life, which makes him worthy to be written about? Plenty. He responded to situations of every distress around him and tried to create happiness in people's lives, which in turn made him happy too.

Having completed master's in social work, George founded 'Hope Society' in 1988, as a student's movement against alcoholism and drug addiction. He established a treatment and rehabilitation centre for alcoholics and drug addicts in Belgaum in 1999, named 'Hope Recovery Centre'. Having expanded it to an integrated eighty-bedded centre for the whole of North Karnataka, the centre has treated over 12,000 people in twenty years.

In 2001, George was appointed as director of Sumanahalli Leprosy Home, the biggest leprosy centre in Asia, located on 63 acres of land leased from the government. He developed Sumanahalli into a world class treatment and rehabilitation centre for leprosy with global collaboration. He converted Sumanahalli campus from being just a leprosy centre to a campus for all social segments who were destitute. People with disabilities were also admitted in the centre for residential care. Those who had become orphans due to leprosy, HIV and disabilities were provided shelter and education through the 'Anugraha Centre', by inviting the Montfort Fathers to take care of them. Street boys were provided a residential training centre through the BOSCO programme of the Salesians. Juvenile delinquents were provided a centre for their renewal by Norbertines Fathers, through their programme called ECHO. From a campus that housed just forty persons when George came as director in 2001, it was converted into a social hub with 200 residential houses in twelve years. During the day, the campus has about 1000 persons. He established a thirty-bedded HIV/AIDS Care Centre called 'Support' in 2004. Support, Belgaum, was established in 2008, which was a fifteen-bedded facility for HIV-affected persons. Both centres together have treated and rehabilitated about 6000 HIV-affected people.

He considers living for fourteen years with the leprosy patients as the best years of his life. People who were considered 'nobody' became 'somebody' due the various initiatives which gave them dignity and value. George captured his experiences at Sumanahalli in his book titled

Empty Nest, which presented the Sumanahalli story of leprosy rehabilitation as a global model. When education was denied for leprosy-affected children in schools, George started St Joseph's School in the campus, which now has 400 students, studying up to class 10.

One of the major achievements of George at Sumanahalli was conceptualising and setting up of the first readymade garments and leather unit in the country with workers who were cured of leprosy, those affected by HIV and persons with disabilities, called Ahalli Fashions. It has been providing training and jobs to 150 people since 2005. In 2003, Sumanahalli won the award from the president of India for Best Employer for Persons with Disabilities.

He established the Child Trust in 2010, to provide home-based care to children with disabilities, providing forty children with wholesome care and education.

India has approximately 15 million blind persons, a whopping one-third of the blind in the world. A good percentage of them can regain sight if cornea is available. Unfortunately, the number of corneas donated in the country is very low, at 50,953 in 2019–2020. It came down to 18,359 in 2020–2021, due to Covid-19. People waste corneas at death by burying or burning them along with their bodies. A person, at death, can provide sight to two people, if they want to. He founded 'Project Vision' in 2013 as global movement for cornea donation. Project Vision has so far inspired 5 lakh persons to pledge their cornea and 5000 people to be Vision Ambassadors through innovative public campaigns, like World Blind Walk. Having conducted over 1000 BlindWalks across five countries in five years, it was become the largest eye donation campaign in the world with 1 lakh participants in 2018, setting a universal record. He also set up Project Vision support groups in the US, Canada, Sri Lanka, Macau, Nepal and Philippines.

Project Vision Rural Eye Care Campus was established in 2016 by George to reach out to the rural poor beyond Bangalore. More than 10,000 cataract operations have been conducted so far, with the support of Catholic Hospital Association of India and CSR support from FNF India.

George believes that giving a house is giving dignity to the homeless. He has so far built 1,500 houses. Recently, he launched a programme called Project Shelter, where he wants 1000 people to contribute just ₹1000 per month to mobilise ₹10 lakh to build a house. He got his dream number of 1000 donors within a week's time. This reiterated Fr George's belief that everyone in the society, however small they may be, can become an agent of change.

George has rushed to every place of disaster to ensure that people are not left alone. He and his team left for Cuddalore, Tamil Nadu, the day after tsunami struck on the 26 December 2004, and worked in seven villages for relief and rehabilitation. Maduvapalam was the first village to go back to fishing in the entire Indian coastland, on the twenty-third day with new boats, as George raised funds for ten boats through his friend, Pradeep Hingorani. The boats were given to the workers as a collective, who became boat owners for the first time, a model followed by all the other NGOs during tsunami rehabilitation work. The Sumanahalli team built 100 houses and provided 100 boats, rebuilding seven villages in their intervention, lasting for two years.

When earthquake rocked Nepal in 2015, his team called 'Bangalore Cares for Nepal' built 600 temporary houses, developing a low-cost model. 65 permanent houses, 2 community halls and a school were constructed over a period of 2 years. Forty students were brought to India and enrolled in professional colleges and on graduation were given placement.

When floods wreaked havoc in Kerala in 2018, his team built 330 temporary houses within three months, mobilising a large number of volunteers. Later on, twenty-five permanent houses were built, each 500 square feet, costing ₹5,00,000.

When Covid-19 struck, George and team moved from place to place, offering support for those trapped at home without food or medicine. Sibu George, coordinator of Hope Society, travelled to Macau in a daring operation with 1 lakh masks, when China was facing lock down. 'Coronacare Life' was set up to give counselling and medical information to Covid-affected people. Doctors and counsellors, who spoke more than twenty world languages, were available in the online platform, set up with the support of Mr Santhosh, founder of 'Billion Lives'. The initiative provided support to 2,20,000 people. DMC India, in association with Corona Care Bangalore, provided large number of oxygen concentrators.

Amid all such uncertainties, something tragic struck our family, as we lost our mother to Covid-19 on 9 June 2020. George set up 'Mother's Meal' in memory of our mother and all mothers. He got a team of people ready and mobilised some funds to launch it as a national movement on 15 August, Independence Day. Our objective was to provide one million meals in one year. I roped in DMCI India to be part of it. Instead of providing one million meals in a year, we provided five million meals in the first year, mostly in India, but in seven other countries as well. Dozens of NGOs across the world collaborated to make it a huge success.

George, along with Sibu George, built a good network of organisations who came together to respond to every disaster. This included Fr Antony (ECHO), Mr M.V. Jose (AIFO), Fr Joseon and Fr Reuben (BREADS) and Mr Vinod and Santhosh (Good Quest Foundation). Along with the network partners,

George developed a large number of individual donors who would support his initiatives.

George and his team reached assistance to Japan, US, Turkey, Syria and Sri Lanka when natural disasters struck them.

George believes that 'everyone has to be within the circle of someone's love.' No one should be left uncared for in this world. There is a need to create a civilisation of love in the world. But he is convinced that no single person can do it alone. It requires the involvement of everyone in the society.

George continues to live among lepers in a tiny room at Sumanahalli. His worldly possessions include two pairs of trousers, three kurtas, a rubber chappal and toiletries. He is richer than most. He has brought incredible happiness into the world.

I keep wondering how one man can do so much.

George proposes the idea of doing an 'Act of Random Kindness' (ARK) every day.

> A random act of kindness by every one of us, every day, could result in incredible change in this world.

29

Lakshmi the Innovator: Educating the District Collector

KOTTAYAM'S MASS CONTACT PROGRAMME, which had the objective of taking the government administration to the people, instead of the citizen having to come to government offices, won the highest award from the United Nations for best governance practice. How did it start?

I did a few innovative things as the district collector, 1988–1991. Kottayam town became the first 100 per cent literate town in the country in 1989, which became a model for the National Literacy Mission. We built a cancer hospital in Kottayam Medical College, with contribution from 8.2 million people. We achieved a quality of health index in Kottayam district better than some of the developed countries.

I have received credit for these. But none of these were my ideas. They were from ordinary citizens. However, I can take credit for one thing: I was willing to listen to people and take their ideas forward.

Here is one such big idea: One day, early morning, an eighty-year-old lady, Lakshmi, was brought to my official residence, by her neighbours. She was furious. She shouted at me: 'This is the third time I am coming to your residence. Coming here is such a struggle. Where were you?' I said: 'I must have gone out on fieldwork.' She was not convinced. To my utter shock, she delivered a punch line: 'Government has given you a car. Why can't you come and see me in my village?' Most collectors might have been offended by such audacity. I just smiled.

Lakshmi set me thinking. Instead of people having to come to the collectorate, we decided to go to the people. That is how the Mass Contact Programme was born in 1988. The idea originated from Lakshmi.

The first programme was held at Vazhoor Panchayat, exactly three months after I took over as district collector. We did not have a name for the programme till then, even though the work was in full swing. We couldn't wait.

While inaugurating the programme, the local MLA, late Kanam Rajendran, christened it as 'Janangalilekku' (To the People).

The procedure we followed was simple. The venue and time of the meeting was announced about two months in advance through the panchayats and the media, both visual and print. It was announced in churches, temples and mosques. Generally, two panchayats were clubbed together and a centrally located school, with large number of rooms, was chosen as the meeting place. Fifteen days' time was generally given, from the date of announcement, for people to submit petitions, which were to be filed in the panchayat offices concerned. Petitioners were given token numbers, with their priority number and the exact time and place where they had to present themselves on the appointed day.

At the first programme, we received only 215 petitions. After a couple of programmes, we started receiving thousands of petitions. In one of the programmes, we received 4,500 representations. Still the collectorate staff managed to read and classify them in two days. I have rarely seen such an efficient government office elsewhere. Once the classification was done, the petitions were forwarded to the district officers with a covering letter from me. The officers were asked to examine these petitions over the next fifteen days and come prepared to deal with them when they came for the programme. On the scheduled day, all the district officers would reach the spot by 9 a.m. We involved the elected people's representatives right from the beginning. All the arrangements were expected to be made by the panchayats themselves.

The inaugural function was kept short and never lasted more than ten minutes. The minister from the area inaugurated the programme by lighting of the lamp; there were no speeches at all. We did not accept fresh petitions at the venue.

Soon after the short inaugural function was over, it was business time and all the departmental officers dispersed to the rooms allotted to them. The petitioners would go to the rooms indicated in the communication sent to them and wait for the officers to call them one by one. All the petitioners connected with a petition would sit around the department officers, discuss and find a feasible solution.

My instruction to the department heads was simple: these petitions had to be disposed of. Officers were encouraged to be positive in their outlook. We would approach the petition with a determination to grant what was asked for. If the application was, say, for a ration card, it had to be given to the petitioner at the programme itself; they cannot be told to collect it from the Taluk Supply Office another day. If for some reason what was requested could not be granted, the officer concerned had to explain in writing why it could not be sanctioned. The petitioner could then appeal to the district collector. The collector would sit along with the officers and the petitioners and decide on the appeal then and there.

At these programmes, special medical camps were organised at the venue itself. All those who came to the programme were encouraged to undergo a medical examination. Free spectacles were distributed. Where follow-up treatment was required, they would be asked to come to the Medical College on the appointed dates.

At 1 p.m. there was a lunch break. The panchayats would arrange lunch for all those who came for the programme, including the petitioners. Officials had lunch with the others. Government officials were not permitted to be involved with organising the lunches.

By 6 p.m., most of the petitions would be disposed of. After this, the winding up programme would start. This was an elaborate function which took about two hours to complete. Every district officer, starting with the ADM, followed by the Deputy SP and other district officers, had to come on the stage and explain the action taken on each petition. MLAs and MPs were allowed to leave only after the programme was over.

During the next three-and-a-half years, Mass Contact Programme was held in all the panchayats. When the entire district was covered once, we ran the programme for a second time.

The system of district collectors going to the villages to help resolve people's problems is not new. It has been there since the British Raj. But somehow the practice does not seem to have produced remarkable results because there was no system of receiving petitions in advance and examining them. No officer can be expected to take a decision on the spot regarding any serious matter which required verification of records. Consequently, the district collectors at these camps generally ended up as 'dak collectors'. 'To the People' was a means by which the official machinery reached out to those it was meant to serve and deliver solutions. At last, their longstanding grievances could be redressed.

No additional expenditure was incurred by the administration for organising these programmes. Therefore, no sanction was necessary from any authority for the purpose. Any other collector of any other district can do the same as effectively as was done at Kottayam.

After I left Kottayam, the programme was discontinued. I think this is a problem seen all the time in the government: successors do not want to continue anything their predecessors did. But some politicians are clever: they look out for things that work and bring them votes. Oomen Chandy, as MLA, had attended many of these programmes, as his constituency was in my district. When he became the chief minister of Kerala, he rang me up and I gave him a briefing. He had the courage to adopt a programme launched by a bureaucrat. Hardly any politician or bureaucrat generally has the courage to do so. The best form of flattery is imitation. He relaunched the programme and called it 'Jana samparka paripadi'. Instead of holding it panchayat-wise, he held it district-wise. He became the most popular chief minister Kerala had, as he was always accessible to people. It was during his tenure that the Mass Contact Programme won the highest UN award. He is fondly remembered.

Long live Lakshmi and the citizen. If only one listens to the citizen, they would have the solutions to most of the problems.

> Good ideas can come from anywhere. Always be open to ideas.

30

The Dog Fighters

On 30 May 2022, Air Commodore Sanjay Sharma and Flying Officer Ananya Sharma, became the first father-daughter fighter pilot duo to fly a formation together, anywhere in the world. They were flying at the Air Force Station at Bedar, Karnataka. When Ananya completed her training flights and started flying solo, Sanjay, who was posted at the Air Headquarters in Delhi, sought for and was granted the permission to fly in formation with his daughter. They took off in separate Hawk 132 fighter aircrafts, flew in formation and did the complicated manoeuvre required of expert fighter pilots. They made history.

In the Republic Day parade on 26 January 2024, in New Delhi, Ananya was one of the two fighter pilots on the tableau, representing the achievements of Indian Air Force. Presidents of India and France and the prime minister of India acknowledged when she passed by in front of them. It was a proud moment for India.

In 2016, Indian Air Force (IAF) started recruiting women fighter pilots into the Air Force. The first three recruits were Mohana Singh Jitarwal, Avani Chaturvedi and Bhawana Kanth. After training they were inducted as solo fighter pilots in 2018. Now there are sixteen women fighter pilots in the IAF.

I met Sanjay Sharma and Ananya Sharma at the India International Centre, Delhi, over a coffee, a day after the Republic Day. Sanjay looked suave in his blue jacket and grey trousers. Ananya looked stunning in a black sweater and jeans; she looked more like a model for one of those high-end brands.

I asked her why she chose to become a pilot.

Her reply: 'My elder sister and I grew up watching our father fly. I thought that what he was doing was exciting. A lot of conversations at home were about flying since I would prod him into telling us about the heroics of fighter pilots. Most of our social interaction was with fighter pilot families, since we lived in Air Force stations. Most of the conversation among pilots was about dog fights between fighter planes during the long history of air warfare. I was so excited about what my father and his fellow pilots did. So I decided early in my life that I wanted to be a fighter pilot. The only problem was that Indian Air Force never recruited women fighter pilots. The few who were recruited since 1994 at best ended up flying transport aircrafts. My father told me, 'Don't worry. It will fall in place.' I chose maths and physics when I went to higher secondary school as I knew that these were pre-requisites to become a pilot. After school, I did B.Tech in Electronics and Communications, knowing very well that a fighter plane has lots of electronics. I did my internship in a couple of consulting firms while doing B.Tech. I was hired through campus recruitment by KPMG, a global consulting firm, in 2019. I worked there for seven months. While working there, I cleared the SSB examination for entry into the Indian Air Force. Later, I also cleared the CPSS examination, which is specifically meant for those who want to pursue military aviation. There was big debate at home and among my colleagues whether it was wise to chuck my job in an elite consulting firm and join the armed forces. I told them that I always wanted to be a fighter pilot. My parents were cool. They always respected my decisions.

'I joined as a flight cadet in 2020 in the flying branch at Hyderabad. There I had to undergo a one-and-half-year intense course. First semester was theoretical, all about military aircrafts. Next two semesters were actual flying. I flew Pilatus. At the end of this intense course, the Trifurcation Board allots us to helicopter, transport and fighter planes based on our aptitude and performance, as evaluated by the flying instructors and the board. I got selected as a fighter pilot. I was hugely excited. From my batch of 120, 48 got selected as fighter pilots.

'I moved to Bidar, where the fighter squadron was based. I was commissioned as a flying officer in 2021. I flew Hawk 132. The training here was for a year. At the end of that, I was assigned to fly Su-30MKI, in 2023. I moved to Pune for Maintenance Conversion Flight course; this is where one learns all about one's assigned fighter aircraft. In 2023, I was posted to the Eastern command of the Indian Air Force. In my station there are two more women course mates of mine as fighter pilots. It is great fun. We get along fabulously well with our male colleagues.'

I asked her if she foresaw any problems being a fighter pilot when she would want to start a family. She said that IAF was accommodative on family matters and does not foresee any problems. She told me that two of her women fighter pilot colleagues were on family way and they were coping up well. Ananya has not decided to settle down but when she takes the call her prospective spouse may be from the armed forces as they understand the ground situation better. She says that even a spouse from outside the military fraternity would be able to cope up with a fighter pilot wife.

I asked her: 'What is your advice to youngsters?'

She replied: 'Whatever aspires you must be pursued with determination and perseverance.'

As the father-daughter fighter pilot duo walked out of the IIC's Lotus restaurant, after an hour-long chat over coffee, I felt that the country was in safe hands, with people like her protecting our country.

Skies are not the limit. Women can do anything.

31

Dark Side of the Moon

On 23 August 2023, 100 crore people awaited to hear the announcement with bated breath, gnawing their finger nails. The Indian Space Research Organisation (ISRO) had successfully landed the uncrewed Chandrayaan-3 on the lunar south pole. The country erupted in cheers. This achievement marked India as the first nation to successfully land a spacecraft on this treacherous and crater-filled regolith, called the dark side of the moon. The mission's success is a testament to the nation's growing capabilities in space exploration and the dedication of its scientists and engineers.

India is among four countries (US, China and Russia) to land on the moon successfully, and the first to do so in the lunar south pole. This was accomplished with a budget of only $1.8 billion in 2018 (growing to $3 billion in 2024). China spends seven times as much, while the US spends thirteen times. Despite the constraints, India demonstrated that advanced capabilities can be achieved if we dream big. 'This is something that nobody has done,' said Benjamin Silverstein, a research analyst for the Space Project at the Carnegie Endowment for International Peace. 'India has demonstrated that not only can they do it in a cost-effective manner, they've demonstrated that they can do something new and different. No one's done it because it's hard.'[1]

Chandrayaan-3 represents the culmination of years of research and development by ISRO. The mission builds upon the legacy of its predecessors, Chandrayaan-1 and Chandrayaan-2, which laid the groundwork for lunar exploration.

Chandrayaan-1, launched in 2008, carried a NASA instrument that played a crucial role in discovering water ice at the lunar poles. This discovery was a significant milestone in lunar science, as it hinted at the possibility of a valuable resource for future human exploration.

Chandrayaan-2, launched in 2019, aimed to further explore the lunar surface with a lander and rover. The initial budget of $59 million had climbed to $136 million, in part because Russia, which had originally agreed to build the lander, pulled out due to the Ukraine war. India decided to do it alone. While the orbiter successfully reached lunar orbit, the lander unfortunately crashed during its descent, couple of kilometres from the lunar surface. 'Fifteen terrifying minutes' was how Kailasavadivoo Sivan, the then chief of ISRO, had described this phase of the landing sequence. His fears were well-founded. Minutes before the expected landing time, at 1.54 a.m. on 7 September, ISRO lost communication with the module. Despite this setback, the mission yielded valuable data and experience that proved instrumental in the development of Chandrayaan-3.

Chandrayaan-3, launched on 14 July 2023, took a fuel-efficient, albeit slower, approach to leave earth's orbit, reaching lunar orbit three weeks later. The poise of Chandrayaan-3's 'automated landing sequence' was striking. From hurtling through space at thousands of kilometres per hour, the spacecraft's descent transformed into a smooth ballet. A final, playful pause, as the system meticulously scanned the landing zone, then did a gentle touchdown on the lunar surface. A rover, named 'Pragyan', or 'wisdom' in Sanskrit, then analysed the chemical makeup of the moon's surface and searched for water over the course of one lunar day, which is equivalent to 14 days on earth. This wasn't just India landing a rover 3,84,633 kilometres away from mission control in Bangalore on the moon; it was a feat of precision, executed with elegance.

The success of Chandrayaan-3 represents a major leap forward in India's space programme, showcasing its technological prowess and bolstering its image as a leading nation in space exploration. This achievement has ignited a sense of national pride and inspired a new generation of scientists and engineers in India. It has fired the imagination of the youth. So far, they had only heard about 'The Dark side of the Moon' by Pink Floyd (It is one of my favourite songs); now they could experience it.

On a global scale, Chandrayaan-3's successful landing on the lunar south pole opens up new frontiers for scientific exploration. The mission's findings have the potential to enhance our understanding of the moon's composition, history and the potential for future human presence. The confirmation of water ice in this region holds particular importance, as it could serve as a vital resource for future lunar habitats, providing drinking water, breathable oxygen, and even rocket fuel. Proponents of lunar settlements and space industrialisation view this ice as a valuable source of essential resources. The region makes an ideal location for establishing a moon base.

The Chandrayaan-3 mission embodies the spirit of scientific inquiry and the importance of learning from both successes and failures. ISRO was more confident with this mission, as it believed that it had learnt from its failures. The ISRO team's ability to meticulously analyse data from the Chandrayaan-2 mission, identify areas for improvement and incorporate those lessons into the design and execution of Chandrayaan-3 is a testament to their dedication and expertise.

Riding high from the success of this mission, India is planning missions to the Sun and Venus in 2024. In 2025, the country plans to launch astronauts on its own rockets.

The success of Chandrayaan-3 is attributable to countless individuals at ISRO. S. Somanath, chairman of ISRO since 2022, played a pivotal role in leading the organisation to this remarkable achievement.

'Science is about learning from past failures. We learnt a lot from our failure, and today, we succeeded,' said the fifty-nine-year-old S. Somanath, a rocket scientist from Aroor, a small town in Kerala. 'As an engineer and scientist, I have a love for rockets. I consider the rocket like a baby, seeing its birth, its growth, its problems of growth, its emotions and developing a deep understanding of its mechanics and dynamics and its life as such,' he said.

Another key member of the project, P. Veeramuthuvel, the project director of Chandrayaan-3, comes from a small family in Tamil Nadu's Villupuram. Other key figures who contributed to the success of Chandrayaan-3 include S. Unnikrishnan Nair, B.N. Ramakrishna, S. Mohana Kumar, M. Sankaran, Kalpana K, Muthayya Vanitha and Ritu Karidhal Srivastava.

Most of the 350-odd engineers who worked on the project, including Somanath, came from unsung engineering colleges in small towns. You don't necessarily have to go to IIT to do innovative things.

> The country can do the impossible when a determined group of people get together with purpose.

32
The Quickgun Commissioner

WHEN I RETURNED FROM Delhi in 2000, I was appointed as Transport Commissioner, Kerala. Within a few months I was transferred as Secretary, Higher Education and Commissioner for Entrance Examinations.

The job of the entrance commissioner was to conduct examinations for admission to medical colleges and engineering colleges. The entrance commissioner's office was on the fifth floor of the Housing Board building at Thiruvananthapuram. We had only twenty-four persons in my staff, including the commissioner. In previous years, it took an average of three months to declare the results. After the results were declared, there would be dozens of litigations in the high court, questioning the legality of the entire process. This would further delay the entire process of admission in colleges. Everybody cursed the entrance commissioner.

The day I assumed office, I had a meeting with my staff. I told them: 'Looks like we have the reputation of being the worst office in the world.' Everybody nodded. I told them: 'Let us make this the best office in Trivandrum.' They all agreed. We got down to working out a system which would be efficient and credible. That was the beginning of a big journey. After one week I told them: 'Let us make this the best office in Kerala.' They nodded. After two weeks I told them: 'Let us make this the best office in India.' They nodded again. After three weeks I told them: 'Let us make this the best office in the world.' They all agreed. The enthusiasm in my office was incredible. Everybody was in office well ahead of schedule and nobody left till late in the evening. I never transferred anybody. I didn't appoint anybody new. All that I got was some new desktop computers.

After much brain storming, we decided that with the existing infrastructure we could bring out the result in ten days, instead of three months! But we didn't inform the outside world, including the minister, as we didn't want to make a commitment on which we could slip up.

When it came to setting the question papers, the system followed earlier was to entrust the job to the Technical Officers in the office, who would scout for question paper setters and arrange the printing. I changed the system. I said that only I would deal with preparation of question papers and printing. I went around the country to the best institutions and the best brains for the job. Nobody in my office would know where I went or whom I contracted. I engaged a new printing press to do the printing, which nobody in the office knew of. I booked the flight tickets and hotels myself so that even my private secretary would not know where I was going. I would take long detour to go to question setters and the printing press. If the question setter was in Delhi, I would never fly directly to Delhi. I would change flight at least twice enroute. On the way from airport to the hotel, I would change the taxi at least thrice so that nobody could tail me. I never stayed at any government establishment. Expenses incurred by the commissioner were not audited and were kept in a sealed cover.

I introduced technology into the Optical Mark Recognition (OMR) sheet by which nobody could decipher the identity of the candidates till an hour before the results were to be published. This plugged the possibility of any manipulation of the results.

The examinations went smoothly. Now began the big job. We decided that we will publish the result within a week. We didn't publicise it. We wanted it to be a surprise. We decided that nobody will go home, except on emergency, till the results were published. I got mattresses, pillows and sheets from my home. I fixed a good music system. I arranged for the best mutton biryani and ice cream in town to be served. It was fun. It was like a celebration.

Our scanning machine had the capacity to scan 10,000 OMR sheets an hour. So theoretically, we could complete the scanning of OMR sheets in less than two days. Everybody in the office had an assigned task. My job was just to be around all the time and make sure that the assigned job was done by everyone on time. I slept maybe around three hours a day on the divan in my office.

When we declared the results on the 7th day, it was a shock for everyone. The previous year, it had taken three months. Six newspapers wrote editorials on the 'miracle' we accomplished. Television channels ran stories about the 'magic'. My staff became horoes overnight. From being nobodies, they became the symbol of a new culture.

Throughout the month-long counselling, where students got their college allocation, I was there at the counselling centre, morning till night. I spoke to every student and parent.

That was just the beginning. My office became much more confident with the next examination. We declared the results of the entrance examination for the postgraduate course in medicine and surgery on the second day. Finally, we declared the results of the entrance examination for super specialty in medicine and surgery on the same day; examination was in the morning and the results were published in the evening.

What did I bring to that office? It was simple – I dreamt big and shared the dream with my people. We worked hard to realise the dream. Nothing more. Anybody can do what we did, provided that they are willing to dream, share the dream and work hard. That is the small secret of success. No big deal.

In the years to come, my successor Commissioners tried to match up to what we did. Many of them did a good job.

A few weeks after this, election to the Kerala Assembly was held and a new government came to power. One day, I got a call from the education minister's office that the minister would like to meet me.[1] I went. He led me into the chamber at the back of the office. There was a middle-aged man seated there when I entered. He handed over some paper to the minister and whispered something into his ear. The minister handed over the paper to me. He said: 'This man's son does not have a good enough rank in the medical entrance examination to get into a medical college. If you can replace the income certificate of the family with this fresh one, he will get into the backward category and get into a medical college. Please do it.' I told him: 'Minister, no certificate can be accepted after the last date for submission of application. It cannot be done.' The minister said: 'Just the two of us would know.' I retorted: 'That is precisely why an IAS officer is in this job, to ensure that it does not happen.' He insisted. I told him: 'It would be criminal to do it.' He didn't give up: 'It must be done.' I told him: 'Whoever does this is a criminal.' I walked out. Next morning, in the cabinet meeting, chaired by Chief Minister A.K. Antony (Some call him Saint Antony), the first item taken up as out of agenda was my transfer. I was exiled as land use commissioner in Vikas Bhavan, with zero work. My office room was the size of a toilet. I was there for four years.

From that tiny office we did a bit of a revolution. We became the voice for environmental protection. Based on our massive campaign, rainwater harvesting became a citizen's movement. Kerala's leading newspaper, *Malayala Manorama*, made it into a people's campaign. Eventually, legislation was passed by the state making rainwater harvesting a mandatory requirement on buildings.

The size of the office is immaterial. We can do miracles from anywhere.

Shared dreams lead to determination.

33

Sweeping in Change

THE RANKING FOR THE cleanest city in the country, along with the Swachh Survekshan Award, went to Indore in 2023. Indore has held the title of being India's cleanest city for seven consecutive years. It became the only city to win a seven-star rating in garbage management.

Indore is the story of three enterprising people: Manish Singh and Asheesh Singh, both former municipal commissioners of Indore, and Mayor Malini Laxman Singh Gaur.

I have been visiting Indore since 1993, to speak to children at the Universal Solidarity Movement (USM) on the invitation of Fr Varghese Alangadan, who passed away recently. USM has trained hundreds of thousands of children in leadership, who have done remarkably well for themselves and the country. I loved the interaction with children. But I dreaded the thought of being in Indore, as the city had the reputation of being the dirtiest city in the country.

How did this unclean city become the cleanest and keep that tag for seven years on the trot?

Ideally, a city is deemed to be clean if it fulfils the following four parameters:

1. 100 per cent sewerage system with recycling of treated sewage.
2. 100 per cent solid waste management system with total recycling of waste products.
3. Effective drainage system coupled with water harvesting of rainfall run off.

4. Daily sweeping of roads and streets ensuring zero spread of solid waste.

Indore fulfils all these parameters, 90–95 per cent.

Before the initiative was started, households would dump trash in and around big garbage cans on the road. Private contractors, who were assigned the job on a hefty contract, would pick up the garbage as and when they felt like. They would dump them at designated spaces or wherever they found space. Air, water and soil were being horribly polluted and contaminated.

It called for a huge attitudinal change from the citizens at large for the cleaning programme to succeed. Indore Municipal Corporation (IMC) roped in religious leaders, community leaders, school principals, schoolteachers and non-government organisations to spread awareness about cleanliness.

IMC started garbage collection in 2016 and slowly they asked households to give segregated garbage. There was stiff resistance to the idea. It called for consistent determined action from IMC to ensure that people fell in line. Gautam Kaneria, a garbage van driver says: 'When the waste segregation began, 80 per cent of people would not segregate waste. We would explain to them as to why they had to do this; plead with them. If people repeatedly gave unsegregated trash, we would let our supervisors know and fine those households.' People asked IMC as to why they should take the trouble to do this as IMC was not dealing with the basic issues of mosquitoes and water. To create trust between the citizen and IMC, they started a helpline, where citizens could register their problems, which would be sorted out within forty-eight hours. This created a certain trust in IMC and created a milieu for cooperation between IMC and the citizen. People fell in line and things began to work.

Garbage segregations is in six categories, instead of just two: wet and dry. 1,200 tons of dry waste and 700 tons of wet waste per day is collected and processed in the most scientific manner. Strangely, even with such a large amount of waste generation, there are no garbage bins in the city. It is a novel idea. There are 850 vehicles that collect thrash from homes and businesses and sort them out into six different categories. Garbage is collected from homes once a day and twice a day from businesses. 650 tons of recyclable waste is daily sifted through by 300 workers and two NGOs, Sarthak and Basix; this is sold to recycling industry, generating good money for IMC. 500 tons of organic waste is produced daily, which is converted into compost and sold to farmers. All food outlets separate food waste and it is taken to a collection centre from where an NGO, Swaha, transports it to designated places, for composting and marketing. The amount of waste that is generated is recorded and each eatery has a record of it. Stores pay a fixed charge, based on the weight of the garbage they produce. Non-recyclable waste is used for manufacture of bricks, paver tiles and the rest for road construction. The central waste processing facility is built on what was the largest dumping ground in Indore. A part of the land has been converted into a park.

Garbage pickup trucks have separate compartments for different types of waste. This segregation of waste at the initial stage helped a lot in dealing with it. 'We know the route of every van and the exact time it makes a stop,' says Deepak Kumar, project in charge at the garbage van command centre. These men receive alerts regarding any problems on the route, including breakdown, road closure, etc; they also get live reports on any driver who is absent or late. In 2017–2018, IMC collected ₹27 crore as user fee for waste collection. The bio-CNG plants runs on the wet waste. IMC claims that this is the largest such facility in Asia.

Surat has consistently been bagging the second-cleanest city in the country award for many years. In 2023, it jointly shared the national award for the cleanest city, along with Indore.

Surat has the largest office building in the world in terms of area, beating the Pentagon. It spreads across more than 7.1 million square feet, in 35.5 acres of land. It houses offices of the diamond merchants of Surat, who cut and polish about 90 per cent of the rough diamonds in the world. Surat has also been one of the biggest centres of trade in textiles.

But Surat was not always like this. It used to be one of the dirtiest cities in the world. In spite of being one of the wealthiest municipal bodies in the country, Surat had stinking slums, dirty drains and garbage everywhere. Pneumonic plague descended on the city in 1994 and killed a large number of people. Global attention was focused on the misery of Surat. More than 60 per cent of the citizens fled the city. Surat's economy collapsed. Exports from Surat were banned. Some international flights to India were cancelled as some global media wrote that India at large had plague. People were starving.

That is when S.R. Rao was posted to Surat as its municipal commissioner. When a jeans clad, frail and balding man walked into the municipal commissioners' office, people were not impressed. He got into action straightaway. He was out in the field from the second day. He walked into slums with its slush and garbage and requested his deputies to join him. In a week, he covered most of the filthiest parts of the municipal corporation. He needed cooperation from other government departments. They reluctantly agreed, seeing the enthusiasm of the new commissioner in the first ten days. He got the cleaning staff to be on the job. Garbage began to be removed and parts of the city looked cleaner. Senior officers who never left their air-conditioned chambers were asked to be out in the field to make sure that the job was done. They could not refuse as the commissioner himself was in the field most of the time. Ashwin Mehta, a former deputy commissioner who worked with Rao says: 'After Rao came, a system was put in place and every incumbent had to abide by it. And the first thing Rao did was to ensure that people believed that the municipal corporation existed and worked for them.'

Once the system was put in place, Rao set the target for capital projects. He revised the targets according to the nature of the work. Essentially, all targets' deadlines were halved. From putting in place a garbage clearing citizen, which was citizen centric, to construction of necessary infrastructure, all went hand in hand. From a non-existent sewage system, today 200 kilometres out of the total 204 square kilometres habitable area of Surat, i.e. 98 per cent, has proper sewage system. Before Rao, 85 per cent of the area did not have sewage. When the floods came in 2006, there was no flooding in Surat, as 80 per cent storm water drainage was in place. Most of the city now has piped water. About 60 per cent of people did not have piped drinking water earlier. Most of the slum dwellers have been resettled in pucca houses. A robust public transport system was put in place; even the well-to-do travel use public transport.

Other areas which were key focus of Rao were solid waste management and recycling of sewage water. Vimal Trivedi of the Centre for Social Studies says: 'The SMC started implementing solid waste management strategies from 1997 and by 2004 it was ahead of many cities in India.' The city generates almost 1000 million litres of sewage a day (MLD) and almost all of it goes to the eleven sewage treatment plants, with a capacity to treat 1,200 MLD. The recycled sewage water is being supplied to nearly 130 textile dying houses, at a price. A tertiary treatment plant was set up later, with a capacity of 80 MLD. 'SMC, which earns ₹140 crore by selling recycled waste water to industries, plans to reuse as much as 70 per cent of all sewage water by 2025. We will be supplying over 250 MLD of treated water to industrial giants like Reliance, Essar, L&T, ONGC, NTPC and Gail,' said a SMC official.

Rao came to a ghost city in 1995. He left it as one of the cleanest cities in the world. When he was transferred, the city was in sorrow. He was a bigger hero than any movie actor.

I took my civil service batch of 1979 to Sulthan Bathery in 2023. We were there for a week. My batch had the most incredible holiday of their lives. Though Wayanad is backward in terms of development, geographically it is the most beautiful district, with Idukki, being a close competitor. The Edakkal caves, an hour's drive from Sulthan Bathery, has stone engravings and pictorial writings, dating back more than 10,000 years.

Sulthan Bathery got its name from Tipu Sultan, erstwhile ruler of Mysore, whose artillery and ammunition were located here during his invasion of Malabar region. 'Bathery' is a corrupted form of 'battery'. He also built a fort here, which is in ruins. A police station is located there now.

Sulthan Bathery was also a dirty and filthy little town in the hills till C.K. Sahadevan became the municipal chairman. Sahadevan introduced a series of initiatives in the hill town to tackle waste problem, clean the town and address the bigger challenge of keeping it clean. He started with a mass movement to clean all garbage that had piled up over decades. He got the municipal employees to get down to work. He also got volunteers to join in. It was a mountainous task. After they got rid of the garbage, the total length of the town was divided into segments and each segment was entrusted with a team of municipal cleaners. Citizen committees were formed in each of these segments to ensure that the job was carried out meticulously. Municipal cleaners started their job at 4 a.m. In three hours, they completed their job. By the time the city woke up, the city was spotlessly clean. These cleaners came back in the afternoon at 2 p.m. for a mop up. Every shopkeeper was asked to keep a waste basket in front of the shop and make sure that no one threw anything in front of their shops. All the wastebaskets were emptied and they made sure that there was not even a scrap of rubbish anywhere on the road. One can walk the entire length of the city and one will not find even a shred of paper anywhere on the road or footpaths.

Use of plastic was completely banned. Plastic water bottles were permitted to be sold in the shops, but one will never see an empty plastic bottle thrown on the road anywhere. Once the garbage was removed, he got down to cleaning the drainage. There were thirteen drainages in the city, which were completely clogged. They were cleaned manually and drainage walls were replastered. The municipal cleaners ensured that drainages were never cluttered again. Each cleaner was entrusted with a segment. That way, everybody knew who was responsible for what.

Wild overgrowth of plants and trees along public road was removed. City was given a fresh coat of paint. Close to 10,000 flower pots were placed on the pavements. The city became a riot of colours.

Public toilets were constructed on every street; it is hard to believe how neat and clean they are. Every toilet has a visitors' book where comments and suggestions are written and the municipal chairman would go through it religiously every day and ensure that appropriate action is taken.

A waste management plant has been set up which converts the garbage into manure, which is sold to the public.

All posters and banners were removed promptly and the area sanitised by the people who put them up. If they did not, they would have been penalised heavily. Parking areas are clearly demarcated and no one is permitted to park illegally, however powerful they were. It is the only city in Kerala, possibly the whole of India, where no one can spit in a public place.

Vellore Srinivasan, an engineer, spent most of his life cleaning up Vellore. He calls it 'Garbage to Gold' project. He generates a lot of wealth for the local bodies through his innovative garbage management and has been hired by many state governments.

> Your neighbourhood can be clean if you take the initiative. Collaborate with the local authorities to get your city clean. Generate the least quantity of waste.

34

India: A Global Digital Leader

THE OTHER DAY, MY car ran out of fuel and I had to catch an autorickshaw to the petrol pump to fetch petrol. The auto driver took me to the nearest petrol pump and bought three litres of petrol. I searched for my purse and realised that I had left my purse in my car in panic. Auto driver told me: 'No problem, sir. I will google pay from my account.' I was so greatly relieved. We got back to my car and he helped me pour the fuel into the tank. When I paid him in cash for the trip and the fuel he said: 'Sir, please don't give me cash; I don't have time to go the bank to deposit the money; just scan my UPI code and pay me.' My phone was on UPI platform and the job was done in ten seconds.

Nikhil, the vegetable cart vendor in North Avenue, from whom our help Jyoti buys vegetables, does not accept cash payments any more. He says that cash payments are a headache and a waste of time. He takes payment only on UPI.

My wife's driver, Sunil, gets his salary credited on UPI. He pays his children's school fees digitally.

Most of India, from big businesses to the cart vendors, is on India's digital payment platform, UPI. It is the best digital payment platform in the world.

India is the world's largest digitally connected democracy, with 935 million internet users.[1] Most commerce stores and stalls, from plush glass door outlets to the cotton candy street vendor, adorns a QR code for payment, made possible by the Unified Payments Interface (UPI), part of the Digital

Public Infrastructure (DPI). All e-commerce enterprises are on UPI.

The India Stack or DPI involves a triad of identity, payments and data management. The identity system, named Aadhaar, or 'foundation' is a biometric digital identity system launched in 2010, that has onboarded nearly all of India's 1.4 billion people. When Modi became the prime minister of India in 2014, there was a strong clamour to dump 'Aadhaar' as it was the previous governments' baby. Modi took the bold decision to build on the Aadhaar base and the Unified Payments Interface was born. It enables free, fast account transfers, via fintech apps (e.g., PhonePe, Google Pay). UPI's open architecture lets users switch between providers freely, keeping their transaction history accessible. It utilises QR codes or customisable virtual IDs for quick and secure transactions.

UPI has processed $1 trillion transactions in 2022, equivalent to a third of the country's GDP. The Covid-19 pandemic fuelled the surge of UPI, as people preferred contactless payments. Transaction volume soared, climbing from 17 per cent of digital transactions in 2019 (31 billion) to a dominant 52 per cent share in 2022 (88.4 billion). This growth reflects India's position as a global leader in real-time digital payments, processing nearly 40 per cent of all such transactions worldwide.

UPI has paved the way for greater financial inclusion and hopes to leapfrog the rich nations in fintech lending. Digital transactions create real-time data on businesses and consumer spending. This empowers lenders and insurers to reach a previously excluded population – those lacking traditional financial history or collateral. Lending in India jumped from $9 billion to $270 billion in a decade, as of 2022. The central bank of India has mandated the use of UPI for retailers above a particular size, with zero fees. UPI is now seen as a public utility.

UPI is also expanding abroad. It is integrated with Singapore's payment system, allowing people in India to send remittances for a small fee. India is no longer beholden to the card behemoths like Visa and Mastercard of the West.

All this has led to a direct benefit transfer, along with making available a platform to dispense emergency funds (such as during Covid-19 times) and reduce corruption.

India aims to sell this as a digital offering, which enables a social and civic identity and improve connectedness. It has signed more than 10 MoUs with countries interested in digital cooperation and collaboration on knowledge sharing and replication cum integration of DPI. The Open Network for Digital Commerce, a non-profit developed by the government, help e-commerce vendors work together and to access third party payments. Another NGO service aggregates accounts to standardise financial information to share with lenders that will do away with the loads of loan related papers that are cumbersome and error prone.

The Digital India programme, launched in 2015, aims to make use of digital infrastructure and services to deliver ease of living, ease of doing business and ease of good governance. The expansion of digital infrastructure, including the proliferation of smartphones and affordable internet connectivity, has brought the digital world within reach of millions who were previously excluded. Initiatives like BharatNet, Common Services Centre and Digitalisation of Post Offices aim to connect the country with high-speed internet and digital service delivery centres.

The data management system provides citizens a government vetted documents warehouse, called 'Digilocker', that stores driver's license, tax documents, passport, vaccine reports and more and is linked to the 12-digit Aadhaar number.

Government services, once mired in inefficiencies and delays, have been digitised, making them more accessible, efficient and transparent. Aadhaar has streamlined processes and enabled efficient delivery of welfare schemes and subsidies to those who need them the most. It has led to the proliferation of Aadhar-based platforms, such as Jeevan Pramaan, Biometric Based Attendance System, Aadhaar enabled payment system and many others. Aadhaar-enabled Direct Benefit Transfer has led to the disbursal of government benefits worth ₹38 lakh crore to 47 crore beneficiaries, which led to the saving of ₹3.48 lakh crore to the public exchequer.[2]

Digital governance platforms like Unified Mobile App for New-Age Governance (UMANG), e-Hospital, e-NAM, DIKSHA, Poshan Tracker, MyGov, etc., have further simplified interactions between citizens and the state, saving time and resources for both.

India's vibrant startup ecosystem, comprising 143,000+ startups and 110+ unicorns, is a testament to the creative potential of its youth, who are leveraging technology to solve real-world problems and disrupt traditional industries. From fintech and e-commerce to agri-tech and health-tech, Indian startups are making their mark on the global stage, attracting investments, and generating employment opportunities.

Education, too, has undergone a digital makeover, with e-learning platforms revolutionising the way knowledge is imparted and accessed. PM Vidya comprising digital learning platform, digital classrooms, massive online open courses, and virtual labs have made quality education more inclusive and flexible, transcending geographical barriers and empowering learners of all ages.

The special focus of Digital India for the welfare of the farmer community involves Soil Health Card, e-National Agricultural Market (e-NAM), M-KISAN, PMKISAN, Pradhan Mantri Fasal Bima Yojana (Crop Insurance), Pesticide Registration System, Integrated Fertilizer

Management System, Plant Quarantine Information System, etc. PMKISAN has delivered direct transfer of benefits to over 10 crore farmers and e-NAM has integrated 1,389 agricultural markets, spread over 23 states and 4 union territories.

Digital India is also leading the digital revolution with focus on electronics. Indian electronics sector has seen growth of mobile and component manufacturing units from 2 in 2014 to over 250 in 2024, and this has made India self-reliant in mobile manufacturing and emerge as the world's second largest manufacturer and net exporter.

As India, which has gained full digital momentum now, strides confidently into the digital age, the vision of a New India, powered by technology and innovation, is fast becoming a reality. With the right policies and investments, India has the potential to emerge as a global leader in the digital economy, driving growth, prosperity, and social progress for generations to come. India is poised to seize possibilities created by this digital frontier.

> We can be global leaders in chosen areas, given our inherent strength.

35

Jadav Payeng: A Beacon of Hope for the Planet

THE EARTH, OUR ONLY home, is going through a big change – its climate is changing faster than ever before. This change isn't small; it's a big deal that affects the whole world. The weather is becoming more extreme, with heatwaves, storms and floods happening in places they never did before. This is all because of climate change, which is caused by humans releasing gases like carbon dioxide into the air. These gases act like a blanket around Earth, trapping heat from the sun and making the planet warmer. This is called global warming, and it's causing temperatures to rise, which leads to all kinds of problems for people, animals and our environment.

As per the 'State of the Global Air Report' (SoGA), published in the third week of June 2024, 8.1 million people died of air pollution in a year, out of which 7,09,000 were children below the age of five. In India, 2.1 million people died due to the same cause, out of which 1,69,400 were children below the age of five.

While big changes are needed to fight climate change, often small actions matter the most. One person who has shown the way is Jadav Payeng, a farmer in Assam, India.[1] Jadav saw that the land near his home, along the Brahmaputra River, was turning into a desert and the trees were disappearing. Animals were losing their homes, and the river was flooding more often. Instead of just watching,

Jadav decided to take action. Every day, for over forty years, he planted trees on a barren sandbar along the river. His hard work turned that once barren land into a thriving forest, spanning over 1,360 acres. Now, elephants, tigers, and many other animals live there, thanks to Jadav's dedication to nature. His dedication shows how much impact one person's actions can make on our planet.

R.K. Nair, from Kasargod in Kerala, who has settled down in Gujarat, created 88 mini forests in 12 states, by planting 16.5 lakh trees. For the remembrance of the 2001 earthquake victims, he has planted 2,23,000 trees in Kutch. He created 'Shaheed Van', in remembrance of Pulwama martyrs from the terrorist attack, by planting 40,000 trees. 1,20,000 trees were planted on Nargol beach.[2] Children all over the world are speaking up about climate change because they know that it is their future that is at stake. They are telling us about the melting ice in the Arctic and Antarctica, which is causing sea levels to rise. This puts coastal cities and islands at risk of flooding. They are also talking about extreme weather events, like hurricanes and wildfires, which are becoming more frequent and severe, because of climate change. These voices remind us that what we do now affects the world they inherited.

But it is unfortunate that not everyone agrees about climate change. Some people and leaders think that it's not a big deal or that it's just politics. But some countries understand that climate change is a huge threat to people's lives and safety, especially for small islands and coastal areas. They are leading efforts to protect these vulnerable places, through initiatives like India's 'Infrastructure for Resilient Island States'. This shows how leaders can take action to help countries most at risk from climate change.

Another big issue in the world is who should pay to fix climate change and reduce our carbon emissions. To become carbon neutral by 2070, we need to spend trillions of dollars. It was agreed that $100 billion would be raised annually. Nothing much has come into the kitty. Developing countries say that rich countries, who became wealthy by polluting, should pay the most. They also need help with technology and money to fight climate change. Global South has argued that rich countries should give 2 per cent of their income to developing countries so that they can take effective action. They have also been demanding technology transfer so that cleaner technology can be used. But many Western countries are hesitant to do either. Some countries that make money from fossil fuels do not want to switch to cleaner energy sources, even though the climate meeting in Dubai in 2023 hinted at the need for change.

In this midst of all this confusion surrounding climate change, the bigger question is whether we the citizens can help solve the problem too. Can we make a difference? I believe that the power to fight climate change is in our hands. We can stop this trend. Jadav Payeng's and Nair's stories remind us that climate change affects us all, and we must not ignore it. Let their stories inspire us to do our part for the planet. Simple things, like using less energy at home, walking or biking instead of driving, and not wasting things, can add up to make a big difference. Farmers can contribute greatly by not burning crop residues. Taking care of our planet is important for everyone. If each of us does our bit, we can keep Earth healthy for ourselves and for future generations.

The plastic industry is an example of how human activities can harm our environment. Much of this plastic ends up in oceans and land, harming animals and polluting our food and water. Even though people know about these problems, our ways of recycling aren't good enough. Most plastic waste ends up in landfills, incinerators, or nature, making pollution worse. Burning plastic in incinerators releases toxic gases, which are harmful. Recycling is supposed to help, but less than 2 per cent of plastic gets recycled properly. Often, it's 'downcycled' or thrown away incorrectly, adding to the pollution. None of these methods alone can solve the problem.

Plastic pollution affects the air we breathe, the water we drink and the food we eat. Animals and plants suffer the most. While development is important, it shouldn't harm our planet. But the reality is that the companies, making plastic from oil and gas, have increased production. This excess plastic is often sent to markets in Asia, Africa and Latin America, driven more by profit than real demand. This link between fossil fuels and plastic production not only damages the environment but also makes it harder to fight climate change.

Big challenges, like climate change, can sometimes make us feel powerless. But there's hope. Every small action we take can make a big difference. Whether it's using less plastic, supporting businesses that care about the environment or sharing about climate change on social media, our actions matter. When we work together, we can protect our planet and make a better future for everyone. Jadav Payeng's story shows us that one person can make a big difference. Let's follow his example and work together for a sustainable future. It starts with thinking about how our choices affect nature every day.

Here are a few things you can do straight away:

Saving Energy at Home: Our homes use lots of energy. Using energy-saving light bulbs and appliances helps, even if they cost a bit more. Adjusting your thermostat and using solar energy when possible saves energy too. Switch off lights and equipment when not needed.

Choosing Transportation: Cars create lots of pollution. Walking, biking, or using buses and trains, instead of driving, cuts down on pollution and keeps us healthier. If you need to drive, choose a car that uses less fuel.

Shopping Wisely: Before buying something new, ask if you really need it. We buy so much that is unnecessary. Choose things that are well-made and last a long time. Look for products with less packaging, which don't harm nature. Fixing things, instead of throwing them away, helps too.

Travelling Smart: Air travel adds a lot of carbon to the air. If you can, fly less often. Pick airlines that care about the environment. For short trips, using trains or buses is better for nature. Consider vacationing closer to home or in ways that don't harm nature.

Supporting Green Businesses: Where we spend our money makes a difference. Look for companies that help nature. Buy from places that use less energy, recycle and take care of the Earth. By supporting these businesses, we show that we want things done in a way that doesn't harm nature.

Starting with what we can do ourselves is important. But when we all work together, we can make even bigger changes. We can help in our neighbourhood by buying food from local farmers, planting trees, growing our own food, using public transportation, or joining community gardens. Supporting businesses that care about nature and sharing good ideas on social media also makes a difference. Every small thing we do can inspire others and lead to big changes.

Climate change is a big problem, but we can fix it if we all take responsibility and make good choices every day. Small steps really do add up. When people all over the world take action, we can make a big difference for our planet and for the future. Let's work together to create a world where people and nature can live together in a healthy way.

Each person can make a big difference to planet Earth. All of us should do our part. Walk, bike, take the bus or train. Use less plastic. Plant a tree every year on your birthday.

36

How to Make the Best Use of Time

LIFE IS SHORT. WE have only x minutes in our lives. The bulk of the time of one's life is spent sleeping, waking up, eating, entertaining, exercising, and doing a million other things, depending on one's interests in life. One of the most critical decisions one has to take in life is to optimise time.

I have been pretty successful in managing time. I always operated within a timeframe and it was critical for my success. I will tell you how I did it and how I still manage to do it. The first thing that I decided was what I wanted to achieve and within what timeframe. When I went to college, I wanted to be good in so many things. But my track record in school was not good. I had to work so much harder than my classmates in college. I had to plan every step with weekly and monthly targets for each of my goals and stick to that. After college, I had decided that I wanted to be an IAS officer, and that too within a year. First of all, getting into the IAS was one in a million chance. But I decided that I wanted to be there for sure. I have mentioned in chapter two how I did it.

Prioritising tasks in one's day is crucial. Every evening, I write down in the diary all the tasks to be done the next day. Then I prioritise them and give each item a serial number in order of priority. The most important items will come on top. Once a task is completed, I cross it out so that I know that it has been done. I did this as a student, as an IAS officer and as a politician.

I always stick to the schedule. If I have scheduled a task to be completed in one hour, I must complete it in one hour. However late I get in the evening, I go to bed only after finishing what's in the timetable. If some emergency comes up and I have to skip a few things, I schedule them for the next day, as priority.

I would take a break every two hours to stretch and breath some fresh air.

To optimise time, one needs to keep away all the distractions when one is studying or doing anything serious. Thank God there were no mobile or television to distract when I was in college and later when I was preparing for the IAS. Mobile phones can be a great blessing and a curse, depending on the way one handles it. It makes communication so much easier. With internet on the mobile, one can be so much more productive. But it can also be the biggest time killer and brain buster. These days when I work, I keep my mobile on silent. I access it every two hours to see the missed calls and return the calls. In the near future, I intend to check WhatsApp messages only twice a day. People whose nature of job requires them to be on the mobile all the time have to schedule it differently. In my house, nobody is allowed to bring the mobile to the dining table. Nobody is allowed to pull out the mobile at a restaurant.

To optimise time, we need to be sure about how we handle social media. Social media has its positive uses, especially for a government organisation which is reaching out to people with its programmes. It is also useful for marketing of products and services. But frankly, I think it is the biggest curse for school and college students for multiple reasons. Some of the biggest social influencers on YouTube, TikTok, Instagram, etc. are gasbags. They peddle ridiculous stuff, which unfortunately is believed to be the truth, which is extremely harmful. Social media is the biggest destroyer of self-esteem. To catch up with one's classmates, one is forced to be on Facebook, Instagram and many more applications, posting selfies and waiting for likes. If you get less likes you are wrecked. Half the guys out there are trying to bully you. You have no clue how to handle it.

What I am going to tell you next might sound cruel. But if you want to save your kids from being wrecked, there are few choices before you.

My advice to parents: do not give mobiles to school kids. You are permitting your kids watch videos on mobiles so that they will leave you alone. Give them your mobile for an hour, if they insist, when they get to high school. Till they graduate from high school, don't let them have a social media account. Limit the Wi-Fi to the living room. Let them access the net from a common area instead of the secrecy of their rooms. When their brains are still developing, and their thinking process is in a flux, please don't wreck their brains. But before you do all this to your kids, you parents teach yourself how to control your phone time. No point trying to discipline your kids unless you discipline yourself. Put that instrument aside and spend more time with family.

My advice to school kids: just keep it away. Don't ruin your brain and your soul. Your brain is still developing till you are eighteen. Social media will hinder brain development. You will never learn to discover knowledge because social media pretends to give it to you in a capsule. You will possibly never know the truth because most of what social media tells you is untruth. There is a lot of dirty stuff out there on social media. You don't need social media to make friends. There are plenty of smart kids out there in your school.

I don't know how many parents can do this. I am conscious that I will be declared an enemy both by parents and school kids. Let it be.

Learn the art of getting to the crux of the matter. Don't get lost in the forest. After you read a chapter, learn to reduce it to a paragraph. When you finish a book, reduce it to a page. When you are faced with a problem, get to the heart of the issue and the solution will emerge easily.

Be punctual. I have never been late for any function in forty-five years of public life. I am obsessed with punctuality. Since I am punctual, others also make a great effort to be punctual. Being punctual is my way of telling others that I respect them. Unless one gives respect, one can't expect respect from others.

Optimising time does not mean that one spends time only on study and work. Evey person should have a bucket list of interesting things to do in life, other than work and study. There are four things I do every day. I go for a jog. I have been doing 5 kilometres every day, winter and summer. Actually, my biggest thinking time is my jogging time.

I listen to music every day before I go to bed, however late I am in getting home. I use my headphones, so that I don't disturb others. I listen to my old-time favourites: Beatles, Pink Floyd, Bob Dylan, Jim Reeves, Neil Diamond, etc. Sometimes, I listen to heavy metal, as well. I read every day. However late I am, I still have to read something more than just newspapers, before I go to bed.

After everybody has gone to sleep, I spend ten minutes to think. Some call it meditation. It is for looking back at my day to evaluate if I could have done better. It is also the time to plan for tomorrow.

We must get our children to play at least one game at school and in the neighbourhood. That is what builds character.

One of the biggest time wasters are people who pretend to be friends. I give a lot of priority for time with friends. I do not waste time on negative people. I do not waste time on people who put me down. Avoid them.

Yes, one needs to hang out. Even when I was preparing for the IAS examinations, I always kept time to hang out with friends. One also should spend time in solitude. Spend time with pets. They will teach us the meaning of love and loyalty.

One needs to find plenty of time every day without fail for one's family, especially growing up children. Talk about their day, about their friends and about their teenage crushes. Keep your mobile phones away when you spend time with family. Everything else can possibly wait. I played cricket with my kids and took them out roller skating on weekends. Teenage children also need to make time to spend with parents. With all the digital gadgets, it is tough to find time for parents.

For those at work, one of the biggest time wasters are meetings, especially in government offices. My policy was simple: no meeting will be more than twenty-nine minutes. This ensured that everybody came prepared for the meeting with solutions. After every meeting, I kept at least fifteen minutes for visitors and for returning calls. I always found time to take calls from the public. Even as minister, I took all my calls. There was not one message I didn't respond to. I always found time, even when I was sleeping four hours a day.

As one grows older, it is easy to retire, stay home and watch endless serials on TV. It could be so much more satisfying if one were to get out of home and do something which adds a little more meaning to life, apart from watching serials.

We are here to be happy. Happiness depends on how we are able to optimise time and add meaning to every minute of our lives. If you look at the lives of all highly successful people, we will find one thing in common: they optimised their time.

Life is short. Use the hours and minutes meaningfully. Plan your life and stick to the schedule.

37

Cochin International Airport: Doing the Impossible

Ever heard of a district collector building one of the biggest airports in the country, with crowdfunding?

The new Cochin International Airport in Nedumbassery was declared open on 25 May 1999. The credit for this remarkable achievement belongs to V.J. Kurian.

The history of Cochin International Airport is intrinsically intertwined with the story of V.J. Kurian, who relentlessly fought against all odds, to accomplish what others of his era could hardly envision. An IAS officer of the 1983 batch, it was Kurian's visionary zeal and his ability to dream the 'impossible' that led to the novel concept of People's Airport, which eventually turned out to be a huge success.

In 1992, Cochin Airport was no more than a vision of one individual. V.J. Kurian was serving as the district collector of Ernakulam. Since the naval airport at Cochin could not be used further as a civilian airport, the government of Kerala was advised to identify a suitable location for constructing a new greenfield airport at Cochin. Kurian voluntarily assumed this responsibility, fully aware that without immediate action Cochin faced the risk of being completely wiped out of the aviation map of India.

Kurian explored several locations in and around Cochin and narrowed in on Nedumbassery, about 30 kilometres north of Cochin. This decision was primarily influenced by its strategic positioning, offering convenient access to both the railway line and national highway.

National Airport Authority, due to its financial constraints, expressed their inability to invest in the airport project. However, they pledged technical support, which gave confidence to Kurian to take up the challenge of mobilising funds for this mammoth project, which was initially estimated to cost ₹200 crore in 1993.

Since the government of Kerala was also not in a position to take the financial burden of the Airport project, Kurian conceived an innovative idea of developing the airport through a collaborative financial venture, involving airport users, predominantly non-resident Indians, airport service providers, and the government. K. Karunakaran, who served as the chief minister at that time, quickly grasped the immense potential of this concept. Despite staunch opposition from bureaucratic circles, he granted permission to Kurian to proceed with the proposal.

Subsequently, Kochi International Airport Society (KIAS) was established with Chief Minister K. Karunakaran as the chairman and Kurian as director. The initial share capital of KIAS was ₹20,000. By December 1993, KIAS had only mobilised a meagre ₹4 crore, falling significantly short of the ₹200 crore target. Recognising the institutional limitations, in 30 March 1994, Cochin International Airport Ltd (CIAL) was established as a company with an authorised capital of ₹90 crore with Chief Minister K. Karunakaran as its chairman and Kurian as the managing director.

Despite having a core team, mobilisation of funds was the biggest stumbling block. He appointed KITCO, a local consultancy organisation to develop a cost-effective design for the terminal buildings. Although KITCO did not have any previous experience in building an airport, with the support of TEAM CIAL, they did rise to the occasion by preparing a cost-effective design, which was less than one fifth of the estimated cost prepared by a US Consultant.

Land acquisition presented another significant challenge. An area of 1,253 acres of land was required for the project, which belonged to 3,824 landowners and 820 households, who vigorously opposed land acquisition with the active support of local leaders, cutting across party lines. To appease the landowners, a unique rehabilitation package was introduced, offering 242 square metres of developed land free of cost, market rates for land to be acquired, and compensation for their buildings without depreciation. This innovative and liberal rehabilitation package, which was appreciated by the World Bank, worked wonders – a good majority of the land owners came forward for negotiated settlement which sent out a strong message to the public that the project was indeed taking off.

Lack of funds continued to be a major hurdle. No one was willing to risk an investment in the airport project, which was widely believed to be a non-starter. However, at a time when not even an inch of land was acquired, Federal Bank stepped in to lend a helping hand by sanctioning a bridge loan of ₹10 crore. This timely gesture was a confidence builder for the team and the foundation stone for the construction of the airport was finally laid on 21 August 1994.

In 1995, HUDCO sanctioned a term loan amounting to ₹98 crore. Without waiting for the completion of land acquisition, the tender for the 3,400-metre-long runway, the second longest runway after Delhi, was initiated. It was a huge personal risk, but Kurian was convinced that this was the only way to propel his dream project to a 'point of no return'. Meanwhile, construction of critical structures, such as terminal buildings and the air traffic control tower, began in 1996.

By 1997, even though CIAL had obtained possession of a substantial area of land through negotiated settlements, land acquisition continued to be a major cause of concern. Several landowners were still holding on to their property and challenging the entire land acquisition process in the court. Over four hundred cases were filed against CIAL, and there was even an order from the Single Bench of the Hon'ble High Court of Kerala, quashing the entire land acquisition process as null and void. However, CIAL fought all these cases successfully, including a few of them at the Supreme Court of India.

On the 25 May 1999, His Excellency, K.R. Narayanan, Hon'ble President of India, announced the historic opening of the first PPP model airport in India.

CIAL story doesn't end here! Shortly after the inauguration of the airport, Kurian was unceremoniously removed from the organisation, which he had built brick by brick. Between 2000 and 2003, CIAL faced a period of financial turmoil, struggling with significant challenges, as accumulated losses surged to an alarming ₹71 crore. Mounting losses and inadequate cash flow posed challenges for meeting its loan repayment obligations. Detractors of the airport project seized this opportunity to intensify their campaign, asserting that CIAL would never turn profitable and would become another 'white elephant' in the state. There was no option but to bring Kurian back. Kurian was able to turnaround the Company within no time. The Company was in profits for the first time, declaring dividend to the shareholders in 2003–2004, proving the sceptics wrong once again. In 2017, a state-of-the-art international terminal, covering 15 lakh square feet, was inaugurated, followed by a new 6 lakh square feet domestic terminal in 2019.

He initiated the establishment of solar power plants at the airport premises. The journey began with a pilot plant of 100 kWp in 2013, and by 2015, Cochin Airport's solar capacity had grown to an impressive 15 mWp, making it the world's first fully solar-powered airport. In recognition of this achievement, CIAL received the highest environmental honour – the Champions of the Earth Award, from the United Nations, in 2018.

During this period, CIAL also forayed into the field of hydropower and completed a 4.5 MW run-of-the-river hydroelectric project in Kozhikode, making it the only airport in the world to own and operate a hydroelectric power plant.

Cochin International Airport, which had its most modest origins in 1999, has achieved numerous commendable milestones over the last 25 years:

1. The traffic through Cochin Airport skyrocketed to 10 million passengers in the fiscal year 2017–2018. Cochin Airport maintains its position as the fourth-largest airport in the country, in terms of international passenger traffic.
2. CIAL presently has an investor base exceeding 19,000 shareholders, from over thirty-two countries. Notably, this accomplishment was realised without resorting to a public issue. The total dividend disbursed to shareholders, including the government of Kerala, which holds a substantial 32 per cent equity, has already surpassed 315 per cent of their initial investment.
3. Employing over 17,000 individuals directly and providing indirect employment to more than 35,000, CIAL stands out as a significant contributor to economic growth and employment opportunities in the state of Kerala.

After nearly two decades of dedicated service as managing director, V.J. Kurian finally bid farewell to CIAL in June 2021. In his current role as the chairman of South Indian Bank, Kurian is steering the institution towards new heights, while keeping his feet firmly on the ground.

Kurian has proved that you can build a world class infrastructure with public support.

> You can do the impossible.

38

Defying the System

THIS IS POSSIBLY THE most radical thing I did in the service; it is possibly the most fruitful one as well, as far as long lasting impact is concerned.

When I became Secretary, Higher Education Dept, Kerala in 2000, over 2 lakh Kerala students were doing engineering, medicine, nursing and MBA outside Kerala, as there were far too few seats in Kerala. Most of them were going to Karnataka, Tamil Nadu and Andhra Pradesh. Some were going abroad as well. While some of these colleges were good, most of them were in deplorable condition. Still, they charged capitation fee. Many of them gave out degrees which were useless. The products were mostly unemployable.

In Kerala, in 2000, there were only 300 seats for MBBS, 3000 seats for engineering, 700 seats for nursing and a few hundred seats for MBA. I told P.J. Joseph, the minister for education, that our children should study here for two reasons: first, the quality of education provided outside was nothing great; second, there was a huge outflow of money from Kerala, without any tangible benefit to the state. In spite of this, for the past forty years, it was the core policy of the LDF and the UDF governments, which have governed Kerala since independence, that they would not allow private professional colleges. Communist alliance (LDF) was in power in Kerala in 2000. Any policy proposal had to be discussed in various party fora and then taken to the

Liaison Committee of the LDF, and if it was cleared by the Committee, it would be taken to the cabinet for approval.

I told P.J. Joseph, who was an intelligent and pragmatic person: 'Sir, our children need to study here and for this we must open up.' The minister said: 'I completely agree with you, but it will never be cleared by the Laison Committee; it will never ever go up to the cabinet.' I told him impetuously: 'Sir, don't our children have the right to study? I have a simple solution: since you cannot approve the idea without the sanction of the cabinet, I, as secretary, will issue the sanction. You don't have to be part of this decision at all. I will take the responsibility for whatever happens.' He said: 'Go ahead.' I was pleasantly shocked and surprised. Mr Joseph was like that.

I issued notice to all the thirty-four applicants who had applied for No Objection Certificate (NOC) from the state government, to appear before me and prove their credentials. AICTE was the authority to grant approval to start engineering colleges in India and they needed an NOC from the state government. I kept the notice a top secret. I kept the hearing at Government Guest House, Kovalam. I told the applicants to keep it confidential. It was in their interest to do so. After hearing them, I recommended NOC to 33 of them. I took the file to the minister. I told the minister: 'This is only for NOC. You can sign it. When the issue of final sanction comes up after approval by AICTE, we will think of taking it up with the cabinet.' He didn't wait for a minute. He signed. I issued the required NOC, and the applications went to AICTE. This was in November 2000.

Three months later, the chief minister got to know about the NOC. He was furious. He brought it before the cabinet the very next day. It was decided to cancel the NOC. The cabinet also wanted I be suspended from service. But P.J. Joseph stood by me. He said: 'He has done something absolutely essential for the state. If you touch him, I will resign from the government.' His threat worked. They decided to spare me for the time being. I am most grateful to Mr P.J. Joseph. The cabinet also directed the chief secretary to go to Delhi with the cabinet decision and meet Mr Natarajan, the chairman of AICTE. I got to know of this. I pre-empted the chief secretary, went to Delhi, met the AICTE Chairman and persuaded him to ignore the objection of the government and grant approval. He was an honest and daring man. He did it. That is how private engineering colleges were set up in Kerala. 13 colleges were started in 2001, and it went up to 150 in ten years. Since private engineering colleges were started in the state, the next government which came to power in a few months had to grant NOC for starting medical colleges in the private sector. Eventually, NOC was granted for starting nursing, MBA and dental colleges. In a few years, we had 2,00,000 seats in engineering, medical, dental, MBA and nursing colleges in Kerala. It brought in investment of thousands of crores into the state. It created thousands of jobs in a job starved state.

Some of the private colleges I started have become some of the best in the country.

Few years later, Ambassador T.P. Sreenivasan, one of the most erudite and competent diplomats India has ever produced, was appointed as the Chairman of Kerala Higher Education Council. He made many sensible suggestions. One of the suggestions was to permit private and foreign universities in Kerala. The student wing of a leading political party beat him up in public. Fast forward twenty years: the same party has now approved the idea of private foreign universities in Kerala.

I have violated many rules as a bureaucrat, whenever I felt it was good for the people. But I think this was the most radical one. I defied the government and got away.

But what I did was completely out of the way, and I won't advise anybody to do what I did, unless they are willing to put their career at stake. However, this is one action that has benefitted the largest number of young people and their families. It gave them hope and a future. Given an opportunity, I will do it all over again.

> Have the courage to take the risk, even when it involves setback to one's career.

39

Introvert to Record-Breaker

Binu Kannanthanam was my neighbour, who lived just 2 kilometres from my house. He walked to school through the footpath next to my house for ten years. He is my first cousin. Yet, I cannot ever recollect Binu dropping by at my home for a visit, not even on festivals. I am sure he did drop by home many times; but I cannot recollect as he made himself invisible. I never had a decent conversation with him as he was the supreme introvert. He kept to himself.

Fast forward to 2017. He broke the Guinness Book World record for the longest nonstop speech ever made in the history of the world: seventy-seven hours, spread over three nights and four days. He began his speech at 8.59 a.m. on Tuesday, 5 September 2017 and concluded at 2 p.m. on Friday, 8 September 2017. He spoke for thirteen hours at a stretch, without taking any break. Representatives of Universal Record Forum were present at Chaitanya Pastoral Centre, Kottayam, where the event took place. After examining all the records, he was given the official recognition by Guinness in 2018. Guinness Records have stringent rules: you cannot rest or sleep; you have to be on your feet; you cannot sit down or lean on anything; you cannot use any prompter or note pads; you cannot repeat the same idea or the same story; there cannot be long pauses between sentences; toilet and food breaks were clearly specified; there must be an audience of at least fifty people throughout the speech.

How could a tongue-tied, shy, introvert kid from a remote village without electricity, become the most talkative person on the planet?

Binu told me: 'I was a very shy child. I walked alone to the school, which was about 3 kilometres from my home. I never participated in any school events. I never took part in any competitions. I never touched a mike. I had a few friends, not even among cousins. I basically stayed home after school hours and had no extracurricular or co-curricular activities. I was an average student.

'Things changed dramatically when I was doing my class 11 (called pre-degree in Kerala). I became member of the National Service Scheme (NSS). The objective of the NSS was to instil a sense of commitment to the development of the country. Every NSS unit had an annual ten-day camp, somewhere in a faraway village, where we had to camp. We would be involved in building houses for the poor, construction of roads, etc. In these camps, the participants had to take the responsibility to run the camp, like cooking food, cleaning, and organising cultural events in the evening. On the first day, duties were being assigned to each student by the camp director. I was given the task of organising cultural events in the evening. I protested; I told the director that I had never been on a stage and had never held a mike; I requested him to assign me to the kitchen; though I had never entered the kitchen in my house, this looked like the only way to get out of the assigned responsibility. Besides, I could have extra helpings of vada and Bonda, my favourite snacks. The director would not relent. He said that one of the objectives of the camp was to get students like me on to the stage so that they could overcome stage fear. I trembled. But I had no option. He told me not to worry and that I would handle it well. It was easy for him to say such things; it was his job; but my heartbeat increased uncontrollably.

'We were out in the village building a house for a poor lady the whole day. I trembled the whole day thinking of the evening. My first day's job at the cultural evening was to give a summary of the day's activities. I was told that it had to be presented in a humorous way. All the participants in the camp were hot-blooded young teenagers. They do plenty of mischief at these camps. I narrated all these mischiefs in my first day's presentation. I got a huge applause. But when I came down from the stage, I got bashed up by the boys; many of the girls began to weep. Though I got bashed up, I just learnt that whatever I said had impact enough to cause violence and tears! I told myself: the mike can be interesting. Next day, I was on the stage again; this time I didn't get bashed up; there were no tears. From that day I loved the mike; I loved the stage. For the rest of my college life, I grabbed it at every opportunity.

'That is when I heard what Abdul Kalam had said: "Dream, dream, dream. Dreams transform into thoughts and thoughts result in action." I dreamt of becoming a great orator. I told myself that I wanted to be the best in the world. I organised my entire life around becoming one, even though I was running a small furniture business in my home town. Waiting for customers, I read all kinds of motivational books, including your book *Making a Difference*. I watched a lot of videos of great orators. I programmed my entire life style towards the goal. I began to exercise so that I would be fit for any task for long hours. I engineered my food habits so that my brain would get the maximum input; most of the time food was rooted grams and passion fruit juice.

'I began running leadership courses in schools and colleges across Kerala. I entrusted my furniture business to a friend. I still owned it. When I told my family that I was going to make an attempt at Guinness Records, they didn't believe me, even though they knew that I was a good orator. I drew up a systematic schedule of preparation. It was tough; I practised for days together without sleep and with minimum but necessary food. Two weeks before the event, I stopped all practice. It was time for introspection and consolidation of thought. I knew I could do it.

'On 5 September 2017, I reached the venue an hour before the scheduled start. My family was with me. Lots of people from my village were there in the audience. The media was there in full strength but were sceptical. I started my speech at 8.59 a.m. on a Tuesday. I didn't take the permissible break often; I drove myself as much as I could in one stretch. All the food I needed was in the fridge. On a cue from me it would be heated; food break was brief and short. After the end of the first day, I felt tired but not exhausted. When it was the usual sleeping time, I felt sleepy. After all, I am a human being. I hung on. At the end of the second day, I felt less exhausted. On the third day I was fine and enthusiastic. When I crossed seventy-five hours, which was the existing Guinness Record, the audience thought that I would stop; but I was pretty clear that I wanted to do another two hours more and hit seventy-seven. I did it. There was a massive applause; the media went crazy. I had to wait for a few months for Guinness to verify and declare me as the record holder in 2018.'

Ever since, Binu has been the most sought-after motivational trainer in Kerala's schools and colleges, including professional colleges; he is also the most expensive trainer in Kerala. His calendar is generally full for the next six months. His favourite audience is school and college kids. He insists that when he speaks both parents and teachers of the institution are present in full strength. He thinks that parents and teachers need to be transformed first for children to be transformed. He also trains civil service aspirants, bureaucrats and police officers. From being an introvert kid, he has become the most talkative and meaningful orator.

He was the chief strategist for all my elections.

Life as a motivational speaker is not necessarily one of poverty. Binu has built a beautiful house on the banks of Manimala River and drives around in a Mercedes Benz and BMW.

From a tongue-tied teenager to the Guinness Book of Records has been a long and arduous journey for Binu. Anybody who is willing to dream big and work on it can do what Binu did. It can be extremely rewarding.

I am not dumb. I have talents. I just need to believe in myself and work on it.

40

Keep Smiling

I LOVE MEETING MY civil service batch mates Sanjeev Nair and his wife Rani over a coffee often at India International Centre, because Sanjeev has the most incredible laughter. It emanates from the heart and reverberates over the four walls of the coffee lounge. Very often, I am embarrassed because the coffee lounge etiquette lays down that one shall not laugh loud. I don't know how Rani tolerated him for 40 years. But I love Sanjeev. He is life. Laughter is life. I love everybody who can laugh their hearts out. Laughter is so therapeutic.

I am a motivational speaker. The most important thing that I keep repeating to my audience is 'SMILE', it costs nothing and solves lots of problems. There is only one weapon to disarm the worst: a gentle harmless smile. It disarms even the most wicked and stone hearted.

Don't ever carry hatred in your soul. No point killing yourself, just because somebody else is mean. The other day, I was watching an interview of Art of Living founder, Sri Sri Ravi Shankar. There was one thing that he said which struck me deeply: 'Keep smiling and make others smile. It is so simple.' I met him in Bangalore, when I went to speak to youngsters there at the national youth meet. His message to the crowd was so simple: 'Be happy and make others happy.' He lives true to his exhortation. He keeps smiling all the time. There are Art of Living centres in over 150 countries. I speak at some of these centres once in a while.

Sadhguru of Isha Foundation, whom I admire a lot for his down to earth teachings and sense of humour, says even in simpler terms: 'Life is ticking away. Smile with your bones. Every moment there are a million miracles happening around you: a flower blossoming, a bird tweeting, a bee humming, a raindrop falling, a snowflake wafting along the clear evening air. There is magic everywhere. If you learn how to live it, life is nothing short of a daily miracle. Smile.' Deeply profound.

The Sermon on the Mount is one of the simplest statements ever made. The message of the Gita and the Quran are pretty simple. A plain smile speaks more than volumes of literature.

We are such a serious species. We refuse to smile. Our jaws are designed to keep a smile on the lips; we have to make such a great effort to be hostile. We do make a great effort at that. We succeed most often. It is natural for children to smile. It is in their DNA. But parents teach them to be hostile. In some countries, it is forbidden to smile at strangers. Why go far, it happens in our neighbourhood as well. Kids are taught to keep a stiff upper lip. Such huge energy is wasted in trying to appear hostile. A smile can bring so much happiness so easily. It can save us so many calories.

Why don't we smile? I think it is due to our inflated ego: I am big, the other is nothing.

The moment I got into the bureaucracy, I decided that I was going to smile my way to hearts, because it costs me nothing. Once in the field, with my first posting as sub collector, I realised that I do not have solutions to all the problems of the world. Once I received somebody with a smile, half the problem was over. When I listened to their problems with all intensity, another 25 per cent of the problem was over. If I could solve the problem, there was unlimited 100 per cent joy.

As managing director of Kerala Milk Federation, selling milk for three years, I found that smiling to customers got us to sell much more milk than any technology or management technique. So, the first commandment to all the milk booths was 'SMILE'. I also earned the big trust of the consumer, when I announced that we would replace any damaged milk without any questions. They didn't have to come back to the milk booth with the damaged milk; we delivered the replacement at home with a big smile, with no questions asked. Our sales took off like never before. Trust the citizen and they trust you.

By the time I became the district collector of Kottayam, smile was the main weapon in my armoury. Of course, I worked extremely hard as well. I would meet people from 6 a.m. at the residence and move to the office by 10. Then it would be an incredible sea of visitors and meetings. I made sure that anybody who ever desired to meet me, met me. I have kept this commitment in forty-five years of public life, even as a union minister; it is not difficult. After every meeting, I reserve ten minutes for the public. My smile brought happiness on the face of lots of people.

Nobody mistook my smile as a sign of weakness. I am known as a tough administrator. Nobody fools around with me at work. Even my ADM would not dare to come to the office late by five minutes.

As the commissioner of DDA, when I was knocking down illegal buildings of the mafia in Delhi, I carried a gun for eight years. Nobody touched an inch of land or laid an illegal brick in Delhi during the five years I was commissioner. I never had to use a bullet. I never would. I never had to suspend or terminate an employee in forty-five years of public service. Once they worked with me, they shared my dream and many of them did a lot better than I did. They all smiled a lot.

When I joined politics, my smile strategy produced immediate results. I was going back to my district fifteen years after moving out as the district collector. They never forgot the smile. They elected me as an independent MLA on the 32nd day. Eventually, I won the best MLA award. I decided that I was going to spend time with them in the villages, listening to their problems with a smile.

As tourism minister of India, I realised that the best weapon in tourism was to smile. I received every visitor with a smile and a hot cup of coffee. Nobody left without either of these. I went around the country and the world, with a big smile, selling India as a great destination. We got to 3rd rank in global tourism, with a gross revenue of $234 billion, employing 81 million people. What did I teach tourism India in the short period I was there: smile and get the customers to smile. Be professional. It worked.

Why do important people refuse to smile?

> Smile, it costs nothing.

41

Avtar Singh Bhasin: Prolific at 89

DURING MY FREQUENT VISITS to the India International Centre, I never missed visiting the Centre's library. In fact, I wrote this book at IIC library. I often noticed an old Sikh, furiously working on his laptop. Slowly I started observing him and found that he rarely raised his head from the laptop. I did not know his age, but he definitely looked more than eighty; though later I found out that he was eighty-nine. That made me more curious, since I never missed him as my visits became more frequent after I demitted the office of union minister and later as an MP. He was sitting at the same desk, day after day, week after week, month after month. Checking with the library staff, I was amazed to learn that he had been coming to the library for almost twenty-five years, never missing a single day, except Sundays, when he takes a day off.

That whetted my appetite to know him more closely. One day, I dared to disturb him and invited him for a cup of coffee for a long chat to know him more intimately. I was surprised that despite his eighty-nine years, he was perfectly fit and frankly did not look more than seventy.

When I asked him the secret of his health, he did not attribute it to any particular reason. He told me an interesting anecdote. The day he retired, on 30 June 1993, and went home, his wife, as was the routine, made tea for him and as he sat down with his wife, she told him with folded hands, affectionately: 'While I would love to spend more time with you, do what you like to do; don't sit at home all day and become an idle person.' He said that she had seen him active all his working life, and she was worried that idleness would destroy his health. He took the advice seriously and left his house routinely around 10 a.m. and didn't return home till evening. After her death in 1996, he started spending more of his time in the library.

Now I started taking greater interest in him and there were frequent coffee sessions, and I got greater insight into his life and interests. I came to know that he has a son and a daughter. His son lives in Singapore and his daughter is settled in Noida. He said that she was always at hand if he ever had a problem of any sort. Luckily, he did not have any major illness and never needed hospitalisation.

I asked him how he got interested in the work he was doing. What he said was fascinating, and I would allow him to speak for himself. Here is his story in his own words:

'As I was retiring from the Indian Foreign Service at sixty, it worried me what I would do to occupy myself, since I would have all the time in the world to myself. One thing I was sure: I would not pick up a new job, whatever the attraction. My needs were few and I found my pension enough to meet the needs of my simple life. My children were all settled, and I had a small DDA flat to live in.

'Mulling over the various options, I decided to do some academic work. I knew that I did not have a talent for any literary work and decided never to attempt one. I knew that I was not a known person, that my writings on political and current issues would not attract any attention. An idea struck me at this stage: Do the kind of work which no one had attempted. I decided that I would document India's foreign relations since independence. It would include all primary and secondary materials; this would be of immense value to the government in the future and would be of great use as raw material for research students and other interested persons across the globe. Such works too would have great value for posterity. The die was cast and I decided to take it up seriously as my new profession, as the post-retirement occupation.

'I first attempted a two-volume study on Nepal and Bangladesh. The success was beyond my expectation, and that was a catalyst for further studies.

'I decided to document India–Sri Lanka relations, where India was seriously involved in the Tamil issue. In 2001, I succeeded in publishing a five-volume study under the title *India–Sri Lanka Relations and Sri Lanka's Ethnic Conflict*, which was a big success. Thereafter, there was no looking back. I produced a five-volume documentary study of India's relations with Bangladesh, Nepal and China. A similar study on India–Pakistan was published in ten volumes.

'Simultaneously, between 2002 and 2013, I published for the Ministry of External Affairs an annual series, India's Foreign Relations, which showcased every activity that any department or ministry of the government of India undertook in foreign domain.

'This meant enormous amount of output: thirty volumes on India's relations with its neighbours and another twelve volumes on foreign relations, altogether forty-two volumes, each containing not less than about a thousand pages.

'These publications have given me some standing and people know me as a serious student of history. I took courage in both hands and started writing on recent events, and published the following books for the general public: *Some Called It Partition, Some Freedom*, *India in Sri Lanka: Between Lion and the Tigers*, *India–Pakistan: Neighbours at Odds* and *Nehru, Tibet and China.* His forthcoming book is *Negotiating India's Landmark Agreements*.

Starting at sixty, Mr Bhasin has produced enormous amount of incredible stuff. I doubt whether any country in the world has such valuable publications, documenting their foreign policy, done by a single person out of passion. It is the most invaluable guide to policy makers in the Ministry of External Affairs and for anyone who is interested in foreign policy analysis.

For most people, life ends at retirement from the office. For bureaucrats, retirement from job is a nightmare. To dream of a life without files and office is unthinkable. Lots of them lead depressed lives.

I have heard of some legends who never retire. Warren Buffet still works at ninety-eight. His legendary advisor since 1978, Charlie Munger, who died at ninety-nine, worked till the end. There are also lots of people who created empires post-retirement. Colonel Sanders founded Kentucky Fried Chicken after sixty. D.C. Kizhakkemuri, the founder of DC Books, started the publishing house after retirement. Ashok Soota, one of the most successful entrepreneurs, is till setting up innovative companies, at eighty-two.

Bhasin's has been a remarkable journey.

> Retirement can be the beginning of a new life. There is no upper age limit for doing meaningful work.

42

Fathima: The Wonder Girl

FATHIMA, BORN ON 25 January 2006, was not like any other baby: she was born blind. Her mother's world collapsed at the news. All the million dreams she had of her baby girl vanished in a split second. It was tragedy at its worst for an ordinary woman from a village. Life crumbled beneath her feet. She was humiliated by all the world around her. She was forced to endure shame from her own family members who wanted nothing to do with her, referring to the baby as a 'cursed child'.

Then the long and arduous journey began. After all, it was her precious child. She was determined to bring her up as best as she could. She decided that both she and the child would be happy in their own world.

The mother raised her child with smiles and laughter. Over time, she grew up to be a young curious toddler, who always loved learning something new every moment, even though it was darkness all around. She grew up as a chirpy kid, who loved to make friends. When the time came for her to begin her education, her parents enrolled her into a school for blind children. She was at the bottom of the class in studies; her teachers expressed their concerns to her parents; they believed that she had no ability to learn; they were of the opinion that the future had nothing in store for her; but, fortunately for her, there were some teachers who took time to get to know her and accept her for who she was. This led the school music teacher to discover her musical talent. She was introduced to the world of music. She started with sa re ga ma … She began to sing. She began to play musical instruments. Over time, she was able to participate in various musical competitions; it was a long time before she emerged as the winner in local competitions. Slowly, Fathima Anshi was known throughout the neighbourhood.

Her life seemed to be moving at a normal pace, within the confines of her school and village, until one day her music teacher informed her of a golden opportunity to sing in an upcoming movie called *At Once* when she was just seven. Her face and voice began to be recognised beyond her village.

Recognising the huge limitations of traditional tools of learning for a blind person, she got introduced into the magic of computer and internet, early in her life. She discovered its unlimited possibilities. She learnt to use every tool available in the digital world. The learning process has been tough; but she enjoyed it greatly as this freed her from dependency. She could be connected with the rest of the world and discover on her own and communicate what she wanted.

Things took an interesting turn as she began growing up into a girl with big dreams and aspirations. She started showing interest in academics. She happened to encounter the world of linguistics, which immediately caught her attention. She was intrigued to learn more about the culture that represented the musical forms that belonged to different corners of the world that she was exposed to; she was obsessed with learning more about the languages in which the music was written. She was fascinated by the sounds they made, the ways in which the words were formed, and the way they were strung together to form something meaningful. Her new passion was learning languages. By the time she was a teenager, she was able to master over ten languages, including foreign languages. As of now, she speaks English, Persian, Turkish, Macedonian, Kurdish, French, and many more. Internet has been her biggest companion on this discovery of languages.

She began to write music and has often tried to incorporate the musical elements of different cultures. She scored A+ in all subjects in class 10 and class 12, by writing her exams with the help of technology and without relying on the help of a scribe. On top of that, she was able to keep winning competitions after competitions in various television musical reality shows, hosted by well-reputed channels. These catapulted her into the limelight. She became the icon of Gen Z.

The government of India honoured her with Shresth Divyang Balika Puraskar in 2023, the highest award for a special child. It was conferred on her by the president of India, Draupadi Murmu. The governor of Kerala also honoured her on 26 January 2023.

She was recently declared as one of the best volunteers of National Service Scheme (NSS). Her desire to join the NSS started when she started interacting with few NSS volunteers from college who had visited her school when she was young; they were involved with building houses for the poor in her village. In school, she was a volunteer of the Junior Red Cross (JRC); as a volunteer, she took as much time as she needed to listen to the grievances faced by the people around her; she helped them in whatever way she could; she entertained them with her music; she helped them to forget their worries.

And now, seventeen years old, she is going strong, trying to reconcile with those who humiliated, bullied and tortured her. She is not bitter towards any of them; but she is a human being too, with her right to feel hurt. I am sure that some of those scars might never disappear fully, because those are engraved deep in her heart. She knows that she has a long way to go and so she has vowed to cling on to the sword of determination to defeat her fears, insecurities, crippling anxiety and everything that prevents her from being where she wants to be. She has now taken it as a mission to meet those who will love, support and stand by her through hard times of her life; they have a special place in her heart.

She wants to reach out to the maximum number of people with her message of goodness. Therefore, she wants to get into the Indian Foreign Service and be India's Ambassador, where she can reach out India's message of vasudhaiva kutumbakam to the world.

She is an ambassador for 'Project Vision', a movement started by Fr George Kannanthanam, to bring vision to the blind, through cornea donation. She travels across the nation urging people to donate their corneas. India has one third of the blind people in the world and a good percentage of them can regain their sight if cornea is made available. She has given a big boost to Project Vision.

Fathima is incredible. She is so full of laughter and joy.

Don't let anything hold you back.

43

Jitender Kumar: A Small Man with a Big Heart

Jitender Kumar is a sewer cleaner in North Avenue, where many of India's Parliament members live. It is next to the Rashtrapati Bhavan, where the president of India lives. He has been a temporary employee with a CPWD contractor for thirteen years. He is not directly employed by the Central Public Works Department (CPWD). For the first ten years he was a sweeper. Two years back he was promoted as a sewer cleaner. His work involves going down into the sewer and removing all the junk from there. For a long time, he went deep into the sewer and spent hours there; every moment he spent there was dangerous. Most sewers emit toxic gas. He doesn't have to go deep into sewer any more as the Supreme Court of India on 20 October 2023 banned local governments from sending people into deep sewers. Whether he goes into the deep sewer or not, he is still a sewer cleaner. His job involves cleaning rotten trash, which people of the capital so generously dump into the sewer. By evening, every cell of his breathes stench. No soap can take off the stench. He wouldn't go home till he has had a shower in the public toilet.

He gets paid ₹15,000 a month. He believes that he is extremely lucky to find a job as a sewer cleaner. He is employed by the CPWD contractor, who is engaged on a year-to-year basis, based on the lowest quotation. Often, the new contractor brings his own employees, mostly from his earlier contract. Recently, the contractor at North Avenue was changed. Jitinder was mortally scared whether the new contractor would retain him or not. He was kind of confident that he would be retained as he is a conscientious worker. He goes beyond his brief in doing his job. Unlike a lot of sewer workers, he actually gets into the sewer. I put in a recommendation to the CPWD engineer to ensure that he is re-hired.

He lives in a 'jugi' in North Avenue, behind the prestigious residence complex of members of Parliament. I also live in North Avenue, in one of those upmarket apartments provided by the Parliament. For those who do not know what a 'jugi' is: it is a shanty built with four bamboo poles as support in four corners, with a plastic sheet as a roof and with discarded sarees covering all around the four poles, for privacy. Sometimes, ten people live in a 100 square feet jugi. One wonders how they manage to cook, sleep and study in such a small space.

Jitender is from Lakshampur village, in Bulandshahr, UP. He is thirty-three. He came to Delhi in 2010. He was nineteen. He had studied up to class 5 in the village school. His father was an agricultural labourer. His father could not afford to teach him any further. He was sent to graze the neighbour's cows, in return for food, and occasionally some small change came his way. His father died three years ago. His mother is an Asha worker. Her job is to take pregnant women to the hospital. Her salary depends on the number of patients she is able to take to the hospital. There is no stable salary.

Jitender has nine siblings. He has helped his brothers financially to complete their school. Two of his brothers, who completed class 10, are living in Delhi in North Avenue. One works in the house of an MP on North Avenue and another one in the MP's canteen in North Avenue. Both live separately in MP's servant's accommodation; but most of the time, they are at Jitender's house for dinner.

His wife, Anita, is from Ahmedghar in Bulandshahr District. She didn't go to school because her parents could not afford to send her to school. She has five siblings. None of them went to school. Her father was a sweeper in the village. He is now seventy and is not working any more. Her mother died three years ago. Anita got married to Jitender 2014. She is a sweeper at the residence of an MP in North Avenue. She gets ₹5,500 a month; the MP's residence provides lunch. They have two children, who are ten and five. Her elder one is studying in the NDMC school nearby in class 4 and the younger one is studying in nursery in the same school. Since it is a government school, there is no tuition fees.

Total income of the family is approximately ₹20,500 per month.

Anita's sister's ten-year-old daughter, Neha, lives with them. She is not going to school as her parents did not send her to school when the time came. Neha's mother died when she was a baby. Her father married again. Jitender is now contemplating how to get her started in a school. She is too old to fit into a nursery class with kids much younger; she is not literate to join a higher class. It is a dilemma.

He has to get his widowed sister married. Her husband died of brain haemorrhage some time back. He had funded her marriage earlier. Her re-marriage is fixed for the end of the month. He has to raise all the money. Jitender's brothers also might help.

Though it is not his job, every day he takes the initiative to ensure that North Avenue is kept clean. He spends at least an hour every day on that.

It is not just money alone that brings happiness. It is his big heart. He is not a small man.

Even with the little you have, you can share.

44

Guns and Roses

I WAS LEADING A HUGE environment rally across Kerala in 2004, as the land use commissioner, when I got a call from the Election Commission of India to go to Madhepura constituency in Bihar, as Observer of the Election Commission of India, for the general election to Parliament. I had three other fellow observers with me, all exceptionally outstanding guys, with backbones.

Before I went to Madhepura, I watched a documentary at home along with my wife, titled *The Gangs of Madhepura*. It was about earlier elections in Madhepura. It was scary. The entire election process was highjacked by rival political gangs, owning allegiance to major political parties. They would terrorise the voters and election officials, beat up and shoot people, capture booths and do everything necessary to win elections.

The major candidates in 2004 were Lalu Prasad Yadav and Sharad Yadav. It was a clash of titans. Lalu Prasad Yadav was chief minister of Bihar many tenures and Sharad Yadav had been union minister multiple times.

After watching the movie, my wife told me: 'Don't try to be a hero at Madhepura. They will chop off your head. Behave yourself.' I told her that I would try to behave myself (It never works). Any case, as a matter of abundant caution, I packed my gun along with the entire collection of bullets, secretly. I had never used a bullet before.

I landed at Patna airport along with the other fellow observers. We drove to Madhepura, 180 kilometres away.

There were no roads. We were bouncing from pothole to pothole during the entire journey. I had never seen anything like this, anywhere in the world. Finally, we arrived at the destination ten hours later, with our bodies completely wrecked. The only silver lining was the government guest house, which had enough rooms and decent food.

In the evening, we decided to take a walk around the town, to breathe some fresh air. We had five policemen accompanying us. When we had walked for almost half an hour, we saw at a distance a big crowd of almost thousand people. As we got closer, we saw a sari-clad lady, making an election speech from an open jeep. Guess who: Rabri Devi, the chief minister of Bihar, wife of Lalu Yadav. She was made chief minister after Lalu was indicted in the cattle feed case and was sent to jail. An illiterate Rabri became the chief minister – from kitchen to the CM's office.

I noticed something odd about the jeep she was in: it had no registration number. I forgot my wife's advice and told my fellow advisers: 'What she is doing is illegal, campaigning from a vehicle without registration. We have to seize the vehicle.' My fellow observers were gutsy guys. They said: 'Let us do it.' We made our way to the jeep. We told Rabri: 'We are observers from the Election Commission of India. We are taking your vehicle into custody as it is not registered.' She protested vehemently: 'I am the chief minister and your Delhi rules won't work here. Leave.' There was slogan shouting against us. In my broken Hindi I tried to explain to the crowd exactly what we were doing. Rabri just watched. She didn't provoke the crowd. The few policemen who were with us formed a ring around us. I called up the district magistrate and asked him to come immediately, with police reinforcement. He told me: 'Sir, this is Madhepura and anything can happen.

I am coming.' It looked like a wait till eternity. But we didn't panic.

The district magistrate arrived in fifteen minutes, with the superintendent of police and a large contingent of police officers. He asked me: 'Sir, is it really necessary? She is the chief minister.' I told him: 'We need to set an example and there is nobody better than the chief minister to begin with.' I should say the DM and SP were pretty gutsy people. DM told the CM: 'Madam, we are taking your vehicle into custody. You may leave.' She protested: 'I will not leave.' He told her: 'If that is so, we will have to take custody of the vehicle, along with you.' She refused to get down. The crowd charged forward and the police had a hard time restraining them. There was a mild lathi charge. Luckily the crowd didn't turn violent. The DM took the vehicle into custody and got a police driver to drive the vehicle to the SP's office, with Rabri sitting in the front seat, most uncomfortably. She could never have imagined that anything like this could happen in the wildest dreams.

News spread like wildfire on the national media that Rabri was detained. Since Madhepura was notorious, national media was there in full strength.

The crowd followed the vehicle to the police station. Rabri refused to leave the vehicle. She sat there, brooding for the next two hours. The size of the crowd increased. But still they were not violent. After two hours, she got down quietly and left. The crowd dispersed. We were so greatly relieved. Lucky to be alive again.

At 3 a.m., there was a knock on my door. It was the one and only Mr Lalu Prasad Yadav. He was quite apologetic. He said: 'I am so sorry to wake you up at night. It is only because it is a real emergency.' I told him: 'No problem, sir. What can I do for you?' He said: 'Alphons saab, what you did with my wife is perfectly fine. I know you have the reputation of being a tough guy. I know that you did a great job as a district collector and as DDA's commissioner. My party will not create any problem in these elections.' I told him: 'Sir, I am here on a simple mission, to ensure that the elections are conducted properly. I will do everything necessary to make sure of that. Thank you very much for your assurance that your party will not create any problems. I will demand the same assurance from Sharad ji as well.'

Over the next month and a half, we observers travelled extensively across the constituency and told people that all of them should come and vote, as there would be no violence and elections would be fair and just.

One week before the elections, we set up barriers to check every vehicle which came in. We ensured that no arms, ammunition or money were carried.

On the election day, not a dog barked in Madhepura. Both Lalu Prasad Yadav and Sharad Yadav kept their word.

Lalu won by 69,987 votes.

After the results were out, Lalu, who was present in the counting station, hugged me. He called Rabri on phone and he passed on the phone to me: 'Alphons ji, please come to our residence in Patna for a meal on the way back to Delhi.' I told her: 'Madam. Thank you very much. Another time.' There would not be another time.

I got away once again, very rash and bold.

We can do a great job even in the most dangerous circumstances.

Understand the spirit of the task you are undertaking and don't get stuck in the technicalities. You can redefine the job.

45

Realise Your Dreams through Hard Work

I HAVE NEVER HEARD of anyone dying of hard work. If you look at the life of successful people, one thing is categorically clear: they all worked hard.

I believe in traditional values of work. If I have succeeded in my life to some measure, it is because I was willing to chase my dreams through extreme hard work. I loved every moment of it. Nothing comes free.

At seventy, I do not have to work so hard; but I love a ten-hour day. Not working kills me.

Is it easy to work hard? It is, when you are passionate about what you want. Work would be terribly boring if one doesn't have the passion.

When I was the commissioner for entrance examinations, Kerala, we had decided that we were going to make our office the best in the world. It is easy to take such a decision. But then how do we make it happen?

It is pretty simple: hard work.

During the G20 summit in Delhi, Amitab Kant, the G20 Sherpa, and his team of officers hardly slept during the final 200 hours, when they were trying hard to arrive at a G20 declaration. They succeeded. Hard work really paid off, big time.

Hard work per se won't produce results; no point working like a donkey; it has to be smart work. How does it differ? Simple: smart work involves the resolve to get something done, with exemplary result in the shortest period. It involves keeping all distractions at bay when we are on the job: mobiles, TV, social media, boyfriends, girlfriends, and a million other things. Have them after you have finished your job.

I believe that the human mind has unlimited capacity to think and innovate. Energy is a state of mind, not of body. The mind can take it for as long as it wants to. The moment the mind decides that enough is enough, the body suddenly collapses. It is like the will to live. I have seen people in the most trying circumstance, deciding to go on and on. I have also seen people in the pink of their health suddenly giving up and their soul shrink into their skins. The body follows the mind.

You don't have to be a monk. Celebrate life. Let your hair down on weekends. Go to an entertainment centre and shake to the rhythm of the universe with your soulmates. Except in critical services, employees should be permitted to be disconnected on weekends. They need time for themselves and their families. But you get that right only if you make that big difference at the work place on working days. We have no right to a free weekend if we haven't worked hard enough on weekdays.

Sometimes, we just need to laze around. Some of us carry too much of the burdens of the society on our shoulders. You need to unwind once in a while and allow yourself to float mentally on the waves of an endless ocean to destinations nowhere. It revitalises the body, mind and the soul. But lazing around also has to be scheduled; it can't be an endless process.

I keep telling my boys that they need to hang out with their friends every day, after sloughing the whole day. You can't just be studying all the time. You can't be hanging out all the time either. You need to take a break once in a while. I am told that many of these tech and consulting companies make their employees slough eighteen hours a day, six days a week; sometimes all the seven days. That is inhuman.

Even when I was studying for the civil service examinations, I would never study for more than eight hours a day. I would take a break every two hours. When I used to feel bored, sitting at the study table, I would walk into the neighbourhood park and study there. With fresh air and the wind blowing on my face, my brain would cool down and I would be so much fresher. I like to hear the birds chirp and the wind blow when I study. I would hang out with friends every day. Every weekend, I would go to a disco. Those who were attending the civil service coaching institute along with me were so scandalised. They couldn't imagine a civil service aspirant, who was supposed to do nothing but study, going to a disco. When the results came, I was there in the civil service, right on top, while most of the others who were so glued to the books were nowhere.

> Work hard, work smart but make sure you take time out for yourself.

46

Mafia Strikes

DELHI AND SURAT WERE struck by plague in 1994. Dozens were dying. There was panic all over. People were leaving the city in droves, bag and baggage, to take refuge in faraway places. Municipal employees, who were to clear the garbage, ran away from their jobs for fear that plague causing rats, which fed on garbage, would bite them. Delhi was a mountain of garbage. If something was not done on a war footing, things would have gone really go out of hand. I was DDA's commissioner and I rang up my friend Anita Pratap and asked her to come home. She was a reputed journalist. We sat with a few friends and racked our brains. We decided to do something different. We decided to register a non-government organisation (NGO), which would do a public awareness programme on the issue. That is how 'Janashakti' was born. It had the who's who of Delhi as members. Even Seshan (former chief election commissioner), Kiren Bedi (former governor of Pondicherry) and Khairnar (former deputy commissioner of Mumbai Municipal Corporation, known as Mumbai's demolition man) were there.

Two days after the registration, members of 'Janasahkti' were on the streets, clearing garbage. We were not large in number. Anita Chauhan, a firebrand who is now settled in Australia, led the operation. We exhorted all the resident's welfare associations to come forward to clean up their colonies. What we did was all over the television and print media. We wanted everybody to feel that there was no reason to panic. We wanted the municipal employees to see that there was no danger in clearing garbage.

On the fourth day, we were at Mayur Vihar Phase 2, East Delhi, with the cleaning operation. We were just fifteen of us from Janashakti. About two dozen people from the local resident's welfare association also joined us. An hour into the cleaning and we were attacked by a mob of over 200 persons, all armed with swords and wooden clubs, led by the local member of the Legislative Assembly (MLA). I had demolished three of his illegal bungalows, as DDA's commissioner. He couldn't get at me when I was at official work. I was protected by the government security forces. Here I was, with my two little kids, wife, my sister, brother-in-law and their little children, who had come to Delhi, holidaying. This was the perfect opportunity to get me and my family. They beat up everybody in sight. My brother-in-law, Davis, tried all the martial art he knew. He held back a dozen of them, single handedly, with some variety of kalaripayattu I had never seen. Finally, his only weapon, a bamboo pole, disintegrated and he had to run for his life. He was beaten black and blue. The kids were in the meanwhile removed to safety.

My security men were armed but I told them not to use their weapons as I was not on official duty. I was out on duty as a responsible citizen, and it would have spoiled the message of the entire operation if a gun was fired.

They beat up my wife and left her for dead. She was in a pool of blood. The criminals went berserk for nearly half an hour. My security men literally dragged me away from the scene and hid me on a roof top. They were doing their duty. I thought that everybody else was dead. I believed that everybody must have been butchered to pieces. I imagined long lines of funeral processions the next day. What else could one imagine in such a situation?

Finally, I managed to get the lieutenant governor of Delhi on the phone, who sent his district police chief immediately to the site. We were escorted out from the place. In the meanwhile, my wife was taken to a hospital by Kiren Sharma, our neighbour from Asiad Village, and the cops in a police vehicle. She survived. It was all over the media by evening. Even the BBC and the CNN had telecast it on prime time. I had over 5000 persons dropping in at my home in Asiad Village. This included my neighbour, Abdul Kalam, who eventually became the president of India.

My parents called me and fired me. My father said: 'You are crazy enough to do anything; no point advising you; but you have no right to drag your family into it; keep them out of it.' I passed on the message to my wife and kids.

Next day, we went cleaning Sastri Nagar. My wife was there, with multiple stiches on her head, in bandage. So were my kids. When we reached Sastri Nagar, thousands of people were there to welcome us and join in the cleaning. Nobody would beat us up any more. If we stayed back home, after getting beaten up, our attackers, the criminals, would have won. When we got out the next day, we were the winners, because we had overcome fear.

But frankly, to be alive is a miracle. I have no clue how just half a dozen of us survived the brutal assault by a few hundred goons. Miracles happen, when we believe in them.

My wife became a social worker after getting beaten up. She went into the biggest slum in Delhi, Nagla Machi, next to Nizamuddin bridge on the Yamuna, and worked there for six years, till we returned to Kerala in 2000, under the banner of Janashakti. She ran a clinic, where we treated approximately 100 patients a day. With a population of 30,000, Nagla Machi did not have a single toilet. She put up a toilet complex. Not one child was going to school. She set up a nursery school and got them enrolled in the municipal school, once they were ready for it. She also opened a tailoring centre, which employed seven persons. She was there every day, from morning till evening. I worked in Nagla Machi for a year, since Kerala government didn't give me a posting once my deputation to Delhi was over.

As a responsible citizen, I believed that it was my duty to take the initiative when the country was in a crisis. I involved my family and my children, as I thought that they also should become socially responsible. We cannot retreat into our cocoon when there is calamity all around and expect others to solve the problem.

> We sometimes have to pay a heavy price for doing the right thing, but it should never stop us from doing what we think is right.

47

Sara, You Are in Our Hearts

THIS IS THE INSPIRING journey of a mother and her special child, who celebrated small milestones as their big victories – tough, yet a rewarding one.

Jayashree and Godwin's love story is a testament to the power of unity amidst diversity. Hailing from different faiths, Jayashree, a Hindu girl, and Godwin, a Christian boy, both born and raised in Delhi, began their journey of love, transcending boundaries. They both wanted a baby girl. Their lives were filled to the brim with the arrival of Sara, their first born, a precious baby girl, in 2006.

As fate would have it, her joy and happiness were short lived. For, after a few hours following her delivery, Jayashree was told that her little angel had to be admitted to the ICU on an emergency. That was day-one of the eighteen days that Sara stayed in the intensive care unit of the city hospital. She insisted on visiting her in the ICU and the hospital team obliged.

Overwhelmed with emotions of shock, sadness, anger and bewilderment, Jayashree wept uncontrollably, reaching out to place her palm on Sara's bare chest. As soon as her hand made a contact, Sara began to cry. The intensity of the moment was unbearable, and Jayashree felt as though she would collapse. Jayashree was rationed to seeing Sara only twice a day. On the third day after Sara's birth, a senior paediatrician visited Jayashree's room with distressing news. The doctor explained that Sara's condition was worsening and suggested the necessity of putting her on a ventilator. He presented them with a choice: opting out of the ventilator meant letting Sara die. She fervently pleaded with the doctors to do everything possible to save Sara's life, regardless of the cost. Sara was placed in the ventilator for a couple of days. Sara rose like a phoenix from the ashes, renewed, revitalised and literally reborn. That was day eighteen of Sara's birth, when Jayashree received the most awaited news from the nurse that she could finally hold her baby without any tubes or injections.

The parents were ecstatic at the prospect of taking Sara home. However, their elation was interrupted by another senior doctor who entered the room and delivered unexpected news. The doctor revealed that while Sara was otherwise doing fine, there might be some delays in her milestones and development. The mention of Sara being a 'special child' caught Jayashree off guard. They were referred to a neurologist, who conducted the required tests and delivered the life-altering news directly: Sara had cerebral palsy, a neurological disorder. This left Jayashree and Godwin reeling, grappling with the profound impact of Sara's diagnosis and the challenges that lay ahead for their daughter. When the doctor shared the prognosis about Sara's short life span on her 26th day, overcome with grief, Jayashree experienced a torrent of emotions that seemed impossible to contain. The world came crashing down when the doctors explained why her daughter would not be able to speak, why her vision would be blurred without any focus, and why she would not be able to perform even the simplest tasks without any support. There was a time when Sara would experience seizures multiple times a day, and Jayashree would frantically rush her to the hospital each time. However, after a year or so, they came to realise that there was very little the doctors could do to alleviate Sara's condition. Being unable to roll, crawl, sit or stand, Sara lay on the bed all through the day staring at the ceiling. As days passed by and Sara grew older, her complications only intensified. Alongside her seizures, she began to develop difficulties with breathing and digestion, often resulting in vomiting blood after meals.

Despite the heartbreaking prognosis, Jayashree clung to the hope that she would hear her daughter call her 'maa' someday. But, alas, fourteen long years passed by, and all that Jayashree received from her daughter was smiles and only smiles, in response to calling her name. Sara found joy in being touched and embraced, despite the pain that wrecked her body. Jayashree often marvelled at how her daughter managed to summon a smile despite the immense suffering she endured. There were countless nights when Sara would struggle to find sleep. One thing that always brought her solace was music. Whenever Jayashree sang for her, Sara would respond with a smile and attempted to produce sounds. Together, they would navigate the complexities of life, embracing the power of love and music as their guiding lights.

In the meanwhile, Ayaan, Sara's little brother walked into their lives, completing the family of four. Ayaan became a catalyst, helping their mother navigate the various challenges that surfaced. He literally took some burden off his parents, making their days together a memorable one.

Among family and close friends, Sara was cherished and embraced for who she was, receiving love and care unconditionally. But stepping into public spaces often brought forth a different reaction. The piercing stares and ignorant glances from strangers felt like daggers to her mother's heart, as if Sara was an alien in their midst. Initially, tears and confrontations were her responses to those who couldn't understand Sara's uniqueness. An incident stands out vividly: a trip to Goa in 2017, where Sara enjoyed her last memorable outing. In a church there, a group of educated tourists surrounded Sara and her mother, their curious stares not masking their judgments. Among them, one dared to question if Sara was a mentally disturbed child and whether she needed any help. 'It's not her that needs help,' Jayasree gently replied, 'perhaps it's you who need to open your mind.' That incident sparked a flame within her, a motivation to initiate awareness in the society about the special needs community.

On 8 April 2020, Sara was gone forever. She was just fourteen.

The choice lay before her: to regard Sara as a personified source of joy and celebration or as a reminder of misery. In the sanctuary of her heart, Sara's mother holds onto the precious fragments of a cherished memory: her daughter's last worn dress, the accessories, and even the sand embedded in the wheels of her wheelchair from the sunny shores of Goa. Three years have passed, yet the dress, accessories, and sand remain nestled in the corners of her life, carrying the weight of irreplaceable memories. Each time she attempts to part with them, she finds herself clinging tighter, as if letting go would sever the final tangible ties to her beloved daughter.

Jayashree and Godwin opted to honour her memory by establishing a foundation in Sara's name. The 'Hrdya Sara Foundation' was born with the mission to support other special children. The Foundation aims to showcase and promote the unique talents of these children. They have done plenty of work. The turnout for the second annual day celebrations of the Foundation spoke volumes about the love people had for other special children like Sara. Witnessing such a substantial gathering was overwhelming, serving as inspiration to further their efforts for the special children and the community at large.

Hrdya Sara Foundation works to instil hope and commitment in a difficult world. They instil hope in distressed children and their families through a series of programmes.

Life will throw all sorts of hurdles in your path but you can find beauty through all of life's struggles.

48

Get Rid of the Cobwebs in Your Mind

What are cobwebs? That is what the spider makes to catch pray. It has layers of inescapable complicated patterns interwoven, from which a pray can never escape.

What's a cobweb in your mind? It is a thinking process by which we make simple things complicated, with the result that nothing good comes out of our brain and heart.

As commissioner of DDA, I wanted to demolish a 2,00,000 square feet illegal building belonging to the mafia in Delhi. Some newspapers called me a 'Miracle Man'. To me it was a simple procedure: knock it down with bulldozers. It was such fun to see a 2,00,000 square feet illegal building turn to dust (I was not a sadist – I was just doing my duty). There were no complications, no cobwebs. But I could as well have sat in my airconditioned room and written a 300-page treatise on why it was impossible to demolish. This is what many bureaucrats do. This is what most commissioners before me and after me did. They were all more brilliant than me.

Passing an examination looks complicated to many. While in school it looked impossible for me to score decent marks. But once I decided to take control of myself, it was pretty simple. Getting frazzled only messes up things.

Everything in life is pretty simple, provided we keep it that way. The universe is pretty straight and simple. The earth spins on an axis and you know exactly where it would be at a particular point of time. The same with the moon. When we plant a seed, we know how long it would take to sprout, grow into a plant, flower and produce. Human beings are so unpredictable. Husbands and wives and children get to know so little about each other because of all the facade that is erected around their beautiful beings.

Why can't we become a little less complicated?

When kids get to school, we 'educate' and get their brains completely muddled. Instead of the straight way, we teach them how to go round and round. It is almost never about them discovering for themselves the straight path.

We got to teach ourselves, our children, our students and those who work with us to get to the core of the issue straight away. Most of the problems arise because we beat around the bush. All this because we have trained ourselves, as well as the government machinery and the corporate sector, to spin the citizen in these cobwebs. Citizen is therefore mortally scared to go to a government office. I never raised a query in my files because basically I hated files on my table. I was always eager to get rid of them at the earliest. I left office every day only after clearing all the files. If I needed any clarification on a file, I would call the officials concerned, write out a detailed note myself and take a decision. My policy was: the buck stops with me. I could go wrong; but I would take a decision. If I was touring and came home late night, I would go to bed only after disposing off the files.

My former boss Ram Jethmalani was a genius at getting to the heart of the issue. You could give him the most complicated legal case, comprising of thousands of pages, and after an hour he could reduce it to one sentence. No wonder, he was considered to be the sharpest criminal lawyer in India.

Entrust any 'complicated' problem to my friend, Amitabh Kant, also from Kerala cadre, and he will find the best global solution. When he speaks, he doesn't miss a comma either. At the end of G20 global leaders meeting in Delhi, it looked impossible to come out with a common declaration in the current global scenario. He and his team spend 200 sleepless nights thrashing out an acceptable declaration. In this scenario, they were in fact unravelling the cobwebs in the complex political scenario.

I see corporations like Tatas, Mahindra, Maruti Suzuki, Tesla, Apple, Nvidia, TSMC and Google, which are able to think with clarity of mind what they want and succeed immensely. Tatas, the salt to aircraft conglomerate, was pretty sure from the beginning that they would do business the right way and be the number one brand in India. Mahindra has been one of the most innovative business houses, producing farm equipment to state-of-the-art SUVs. Maruti Suzuki has the lion's share of passenger cars manufactured in India. RC Bhargava, a young IAS officer, had the guts to quit the service and join what looked like a non-starter then. At eighty-nine, he is still the chairman of Maruti Suzuki. Tesla completely revolutionised the automobile industry by making electric cars an alternative. Apple was intent on producing the most aesthetic and powerful laptops and mobile phones. Nvidia anticipated the AI revolution and made chips that are indispensable. TSMC, a government establishment, supplies state of the art chips to the world. Google created the most sought-after search engine on the internet.

Olympic gold medallist javelin thrower, Neeraj Chopra, has spoken repeatedly about the single-minded focus that got him where he was. World Marathon record holder, Kevin Kiptum, who died in a car crash, came from huge limitations of utter poverty to do something which nobody had ever done, that too at such a young age, because he was clear where he wanted to be and when.

When there are no cobwebs, you will take decisions, plan things, work hard and do things like nobody else has done, leaving you with plenty of time to chase your other passions.

Don't let cobwebs gather around your brain. Think straight. Break down complicated problems into simple issues. Then the solutions will emerge.

49

Politics Can Be Clean

EVERYBODY THINKS THAT POLITICS is dirty. But I always respected politicians as they are the most essential components of a democracy. If there were no politicians, there would be no democracy. I always found time to meet them and listen to them as they represented people. None of them ever made unreasonable demands on me, except once, when I was Kerala's commissioner for entrance examinations.

As a bureaucrat, I have never sought a favour from a politician. I never asked for a posting. I happily accepted whatever was given. Sometimes, I was in the doghouse for long periods. I had never visited a politician at home. This is by and large true of Kerala cadre, IAS, IPS and IFS officers. Almost all of them are politically neutral and honest. But do they produce results?

In 2006, when I was the land revenue commissioner of Kerala, my cousin persuaded me to join politics. I was 52, had a great job and future looked exciting. I loved being in the IAS. I discussed the idea with my wife. She said: 'No way. You have a good job and there is no reason under the sun to quit. And remember that you have no money to play politics. I asked my sons, Akash and Adarsh, who were in college. They said: 'Follow your heart.' My heart was suddenly bit by the political bug.

I spoke to my friend M.A. Baby, an MP from the Marxist Party. I told him that I will not join any political party and would like to contest from Kanjirapply as an independent candidate, if they give me the seat. Mr Baby said: 'Great idea. Let me speak to the party secretary, Pinarayi Vijayan, who is on a Kerala yatra.' He set up a meeting between Mr Vijayan and I at the Alappuzha government guest house. My wife accompanied me. After the formality of greetings, he asked me: 'Baby told me that you are interested in contesting the elections from Kanjirapply. Are you willing?' I said: 'Yes, but only as an independent.' He responded: 'Done.' What is a struggle for many came easy to me, thanks to Mr Vijayan and Mr Baby.

I put in my papers for voluntary retirement from the service the very next day. It was all over the media. People were shocked. They loved me as a bureaucrat and they saw no reason for me to quit and join muddy politics. I told them: 'I want to prove that politics is not dirty. What I did in the bureaucracy, I will do in politics.'

The Left Front organised a huge crowd for filing of my nomination papers. They worked hard for the next one month. I hardly slept for three hours a day. My wife, my boys and relatives did a hard campaign.

Kunjettan lent me part of his large bungalow in the heart of the city for the campaign. He, his wife and children were some of the most gracious people I have ever met all my life.

In my election speeches and media interviews I promised nothing, except to commit that I would be with them, to solve their problems. I told them: 'You have seen me as the district collector here. I have done things and will continue to do so.' My opponents made huge litany of promises.

Election day was all frenzy. I visited a lot of polling booths. From the response on their faces, I knew that I stood a good chance to win.

When the final tally was announced, I won with a huge majority. In Kerala politics independents hardly win. I spent only ₹9 lakh on my entire campaign. Once I got elected, I went on a round of thanksgiving.

A week after I got elected, I moved into a tiny room in the PWD resthouse. I announced that I would be a different kind of people's representative. In Kerala, MPs and MLAs spend 90 per cent of their time attending marriages, funerals, baptisms, first communions and housewarming ceremonies. I said that I would attend none of these. My job would be to bring development to the constituency. People were shocked. 'Doesn't he want to be elected again?' people quizzed. After six months, the same people said: 'Just continue to do what you are doing. We are happy.'

What did I do to change the public perception of the MLA? I was the only MLA in Kerala without a driver. Every week, I would visit a chosen panchayat, along with the panchayat president and members and spend the day there, talking to people to know what they wanted. In five years, I got ₹350 crore into my constituency, which was ten times the amount the chief minister got for his constituency. The finance minister, Thomas Isaac, and the finance secretary, L.C. Goyal, were generous with fund allocations for my constituency. In fact, Thomas Isaac, said in the Assembly: 'Alphons has shown how things can be done, within the limitations of budget constraints.' He could say that only because of our performance on the ground. The mini civil station, which was contracted to be completed in four years, was completed in 427 days. In fact, I conceptualised the design, which was one of the most beautiful buildings in Kerala, with technical inputs from Architect Rajiv, a PWD employee. He was a genius. We completed every bridge in the constituency in 100 days. We made it happen.

I am a motivational speaker. I went to every school and college in the constituency and urged the children to dream big.

I had 100 per cent attendance in the Assembly and in the subject committees. I am not a great orator in Malayalam. But I read a lot, researched hard and made sensible speeches. I made a lot of friends with MLAs, from both the fronts.

I was conferred with the best MLA award in 2009.

By March 2011, almost five years had gone by and it was time for the next Assembly elections. On 16 March, the LDF Laison Committee met and mine was the only candidature announced. In the afternoon, I held a press conference and announced that I was resigning from the Assembly and not contesting the elections. There was such a shock across Kerala. Mr Pinarayi Vijayan, CPM Secretary, called me and said: 'Alphons, you have done good work as an MLA. We are all happy with you. Don't leave. There are positions waiting for you in the next cabinet.' I told him: 'Sir, I am not leaving because I am unhappy. I am leaving because I want bread on every table, I want every child to study and I want a job for everyone, across India.'

I joined the BJP the next day and moved to Delhi to work for the party in the Good Governance cell. I left the Left Front when I would have become a minister in another month and joined the BJP when it was not even remotely in sight of power. I don't think anybody can accuse me of being an opportunist.

In 2017, I was invited by Prime Minister Modi to join the union council of ministers, with independent charge of Tourism. I was also the minister of state for information technology and electronics. As minister, I worked like crazy, sleeping less than an average of four hours a day. I think this is how much a normal minister in Modi government sleeps. I had a team of amazing people in my ministry. We produced fantastic results. During my tenure as minister for tourism, India got to the third rank in tourism revenue, with a gross revenue of $234 billion, employing 81 million people. I loved the work, even though it was only for a period of eighteen months, out of which I was away in Meghalaya for almost four months, as the election 'prabhari' (in-charge) of the state.

After I demitted office after the 2019 elections, I continued being an MP till July 2022. I greatly enjoyed my tenure for four and a half years. I had 100 per cent attendance, both in Parliament and Parliament Committees, except when I was a candidate. I did detailed research on every issue coming up in Parliament and Committees. My Parliament speeches were mostly on economy, budget, education and healthcare. All Parliament speeches are available on YouTube if you wish to take a look.

I learnt a lot from politics. It has made me a better person. I have learnt to listen to people a lot more than before, because I know that I am their last resort. They come to me to find a solution to their problems, after they have tried out all other routes and failed. Therefore, the buck stops with me. I met every visitor who came to meet me, without an appointment. Everybody had my mobile number. I took every call personally, even when I was a minister. It was pretty simple: I would take a ten-minute break after every meeting to return all missed calls. I checked every message myself, took action and reported back to the messenger. I learnt to be patient. I was bit of a loud mouth when I was in the IAS. Once I got into politics, I decided that I had to be careful. Still, I was hauled up a couple of times for speaking out of turn, in the first ten days of becoming a union minister. I learnt my lessons.

I believe that humility has to be at the core of a politician's character, as the people have elected me to be their representative. It is a humbling experience. When God and the citizen entrust me with power and authority, how could I not be humble?

Politics is a lot of hard work. I was a workaholic IAS officer; but as a politician I had to work ten times harder; otherwise, there was no way one was going to win elections. One goes through tremendous amount of physical hardship. I rarely had my lunch as an MLA. I had my five-minute lunch break in the office as a minister. Politicians rarely get any time with family. There are a lot of people who think that politicians make lot of money. I sold nine properties after getting into politics. I have given away most of my money to those in need. I don't even own a studio apartment anywhere in the world. I am destined to live in rented accommodation. I am pretty happy. No regrets. Money has its good uses.

> Good people must get into politics to ensure that politics is clean.

50

Sreeman: The Saviour of Birds

On 17 January 2024, when Prime Minister Modi came to Kerala, there was a special request: he wanted to meet Sreeman Narayan. Why did the prime minister want to meet him?

Sreeman met him at Guruvayur and he gave the prime minister his 100,000th mud pot. Mud pot for what? I will let him to tell you his own story:

'During a bus journey, I observed a bird struggling to fly after falling. Inquiring about its condition, a co-passenger told me that the bird was exhausted due to lack of water, a common occurrence when water sources dry up in summer. This poignant moment stayed with me throughout the rest of my bus journey. It was the first time that I had witnessed such distress, leaving a profound impact on my heart. It was this emotional experience that inspired me to initiate "An Earthen Pot for Life-Giving Water" project. It was inaugurated and blessed by Satguru Mata Amritanandamayi Devi. Mud pots, designed to store drinking water for birds, are provided free of cost. Over ten thousand pieces are distributed each year. This initiative has successfully saved millions of birds.

'The project gained recognition from national and international media, which drew the attention of The Supreme Master Chinghai International Association in Taiwan, which bestowed on me "Shining World Compassion Award". Three years ago, with the active participation of thousands of students from Scouts and Guides, this project expanded throughout Kerala. Two years ago, plans were set in motion to extend the project beyond the borders of Kerala and reach a global scale. During their visit to India, foreign dignitaries receive an earthenware vessel from the Gandhi Ashram at Wardha, provided by me. This is to inspire foreign visitors, including leaders, to initiate the "Earthen Vessel for Living Water" project in their respective countries.

'This year, the number of pots supplied reached one lakh, marking a significant milestone. I am honoured to have the opportunity to directly present the 100,000th pot to the Honourable prime minister of India. During his "Mann Ki Baat" speech on 27 March 2022 (Episode 87), Prime Minister Modi acknowledged and praised both me and the project, emphasising the significant impact. He expressed great surprise, "You would be amazed to know the number of pots distributed by Narayanji: one lakh." Due to the prime minister's recognition, info parks, universities, multinational companies and super-specialty hospitals have incorporated this project in their plan of action. I plan to broaden my initiative to additional locations, with the goal of securing more active participation from society.

'The philosophy guiding these efforts is the belief in vasudhaiva kutumbakam, the belief that the entire universe is one. We exist with mutual support. I have been deeply interested in environmental protection because it is necessary for the survival of all, both animate and inanimate, on the planet. Under the initiative of Vriksha Yajna, I have distributed over 4 lakh fruit saplings free of cost. In my village, I planted over 10,000 mango and jackfruit saplings, known as "Gandhi Trees", by directly visiting households. In a collaborative effort with families, we've established a verbal agreement that for every set of ten fruit trees planted, the fruits of one tree should be left for the birds to alleviate their hunger. This approach aims to address the adverse effects of deforestation on our avian companions.

'Another initiative I have started is "Nadam Nanaykkam Nadakkal Vakkam", which has brought considerable benefits, by introducing the supply of sacred flowers and petals. This programme involves the distribution of saplings, focusing on Tulsi, Chethy and Kooval, directly within the temple premises.

'Having successfully persuaded individuals to embrace a harmonious coexistence with nature, prioritise environmental conservation and abstain from plastic bag usage, I took the initiative to distribute 50,000 cloth bags across my local community and neighbouring villages.

'During Covid-19, I distributed over 1 lakh masks to the impoverished residents of Muppathadam village and its surroundings in Ernakulam district. *Reader's Digest* recognised my efforts, portraying me as a "lockdown hero".

'I purchase medicines every month for impoverished and elderly individuals in the village and neighbouring areas. Furthermore, my hotel, Dwaraka, offers free food to people who are in need every day.'

Sreeman has spent over ₹2.5 crore over the past few years on his philanthropic activities. His son-in-law has told him that when father-in-law runs out of money, he would finance the philanthropic activities. What a son-in-law to have!

Sreeraman has become a national icon, recognised by even the prime minister of India, for doing something as simple as providing drinking water to birds. This world is made a better place through such little acts of kindness by ordinary people.

Keep a mud pot filled with water on our window, terrace and courtyard before we go to school, college or to work so that birds don't go thirsty. Let us leave a bit of food outside our homes for animals on the street.

51

A Little Care Can Save Lives

Piyush Pal, a young promising filmmaker, was riding a motorcycle through Panchsheel Enclave, one of the busiest places in Delhi, when he hit another bike, lost his balance and rammed into a tree at 9.30 p.m. He lay there bleeding, as thousands of vehicles drove past without stopping. Hundreds of pedestrians went past, many of them taking videos of Piyush as he lay there, bleeding profusely. They would have gotten plenty of 'likes'. By evening their accounts would get fatter, courtesy YouTube. Piyush's mobile and laptop were stolen.

Half an hour later, a good Samaritan, Mr Pankaj Jain, stopped his car to check what the commotion was. He recounts: 'He had lost a lot of blood and people who were standing there told me that he was lying there for around half an hour. I asked two or three other people for help to lift him.' They got him into an autorickshaw and took him to a private clinic nearby. It was ill equipped to handle the case. Then they took him to a multi-specialty hospital, about 4 kilometres away, through the heavy traffic. By the time they reached, it was 11 p.m. Though the accident happened at 9.30, the police received a call only at 10.11 p.m. They reached the spot by 10.30 p.m. and by then he was already shifted to the hospital by Pankaj Jain. Two days later Piyush died.

Piyush's friend Swarendu Bose was shocked at the attitude of people. He says: 'The worst part is that for a long time, no one stepped forward to take him to a hospital or help him. The people who finally took him to the hospital told us that bystanders were recording videos and taking selfies but no one was helping him. His mobile and laptop were stolen. His parents were trying to reach him on his phone but the person who took it kept cutting the calls and later switched off the phone. Had someone taken those calls and told the family, things could have been different.'

When the accident happened, Piyush was close to his house in Chittaranjan Park.

Jain lamented: 'Accidents can happen to anyone, anytime. I am grateful to the auto driver who drove as fast as he could.'

Dr Sumit Goyal, senior consultant of Neurosurgery at PSRI Hospital says: 'The patient was brought to the hospital around 11 p.m. He was in a critical condition, with severe head and facial injuries. He was immediately put on ventilator support and medicines were started to stabilise his falling blood pressure. However, with such severe injuries, despite all efforts, he passed away. If he was brought here on time, he might have had a better chance of survival.'

During 2021, a total of 4,12,432 road accidents were reported in India, claiming 1,53,972 lives and causing injuries to 3,84,448 people. The worst affected age group in road accidents is 1–45, which accounts for about 67 per cent of the accidental deaths. At least one of ten people killed in road accidents across the world is from India. A large number of those killed could have been saved if the victims were taken to a hospital on time. Why are they not brought to the hospital on time? Mainly because passersby do not care to stop and report such cases or take the initiative to take them to the hospital.

Two days after the Piyush tragedy, a little kid was saved by a passing motorist in Ponnani, Kerala. A one-and-half-year-old child, residing in a little house on Koppam–Valancherry road, decided to take a walk across the highway. His mother was busy feeding the other children. He took his favourite toy and decided to stroll across the road, as if he owned the entire universe. He reached almost halfway across the road. Lot of cars and motorcycles sped past. Nobody bothered to stop and rescue the kid.

Muzir and his friends were returning from the hospital after visiting Muzir's father, who was under treatment in MES Hospital. Muzir also almost drove past when he noticed the little one walking across the road happily. He slammed the brake right in the middle of the road, ran and grabbed him. Another few seconds and the child might have become yet another number in the list of pedestrians killed on a highway. Muzir had to spend a few minutes, trying to find the child's house. When he handed him over to his mother, there was such a great outpouring of gratitude. Neighbours gathered and thanked Muzir and his friends, Yusuf and Nazaruddin, profusely.

Kumar and his wife struggled to get past a road block due to an accident on the road. They enquired as to why there was the block. Somebody told them that some car had rammed into a bike and the rider was in a bad shape. They honked to get past the jam. They got home to watch their favourite serial. They got a call an hour later from cops that their son had died in a bike accident. They enquired the location where it had happened. It was exactly where they had horned desperately, the accident site. Their world collapsed.

In May 2024, a seventeen-year-old boy in Pune rammed his Porsche into a motorcycle, killing two twenty-four-year-old techies on the spot. The high-end Porsche was on the road for close to three months but did not have a registration plate. The law enforcements agencies decided to turn a blind eye as the car was owned by an influential man. The parents, who gave the vehicle to the kid without a licence, are criminally liable. A massive attempt at cover-up followed.

Why do parents allow their children to drive without a licence? Why do they allow minors to go to bars and then drive, endangering the society at large? This is certainly not responsible parenting.

Many lives can be saved if only we care. Other's lives are as precious as yours. Every time I see an accident I will stop and do the necessary to save lives.

52

Lucky to Be Alive

I ALWAYS LOVED SPEED and imagined I would be a racing driver someday. The first thing I did when I got into the IAS was to learn driving. As sub collector of Munnar, I drove the official jeep, a Willys, quite often as my driver, Mathai, lived far away. I had to drive often during emergency visits to sites of bus accidents even though government officials were forbidden to drive their official vehicles.

Driving in the hills of Munnar was exciting. I still think that the best drive in the world is the Munnar–Thekkady sector. I organised the first car rally in Kerala 'Munnar 500' in 1982, along with the Munnar mela. That is how the outside world, even in Kerala, came to know of Munnar. I did the trail run of 'Munnar 500' myself and made it thirteen minutes faster than the eventual winner. I was fast.

As district collector of Kottayam, I hardly drove because there were two drivers, one from the police and the other a civilian. However, I had to drive once, when my drivers were off on a Sunday, when a communal clash took place at Changanacherry. I was informed by the SP, Rajeevan, one of the finest officers I have known, that the situation was getting out of hand and at any moment police may have to open fire. He said that he was at the site and requested me to come. I didn't wait. I got my police security constable, Simon, to get into the car and we took off. I drove like a man possessed for the next twenty minutes. I drove right into the middle of the crowd. Rajeevan and I negotiated with the warring groups for the next couple of hours and the crowd dispersed. I am glad that I broke the rule that officers should not drive the official vehicle. If I didn't, the situation would have gotten out of control and the police would have opened fire. My life is a litany of breaking rules. However, I never broke the rule for a personal benefit.

When I came to Delhi as the commissioner of DDA, I would go on long drives to Rajasthan in my personal Maruti 800 with my wife and children. We were fascinated with Rajasthan, with its majestic fortresses, music, royalty and colours. What a destination! Eventually, I became an MP from Rajasthan and I was thrilled.

When I quit the IAS in 2006 and became an independent MLA, I bought an SUV, a Scorpio. I was the only MLA in Kerala without a driver. All my friends said that I must keep a driver, as the job of an MLA was really demanding. I didn't.

In 2009, I was driving from Trivandrum to Cochin, a distance of 225 kilometres, on the national highway. It was still a two-lane highway. A friend of mine, Maxi, and his family were supposed to travel with me. But in the morning, they backed out. It was a drive in solitude. When I am driving alone, it is my thinking time. Imagine the whole lot of crazy ideas one can churn in one's mind in four hours. I always take a break halfway through such a long drive for a coffee and to stretch out. It is also the time to return all the missed calls, as I do not take calls when I am driving.

When I reached Ayoor, about half an hour from Cochin, I was overtaking a tourist bus at a fairly decent speed. When I almost completed overtaking, the bus swerved to the right and my vehicle had nowhere to go. It went over the high concrete median, hit the electric pole and turned upside down and headed towards the opposite direction. It was 11.30 a.m., and it was peak traffic time. Imagine what could have gone through my mind? One thing I knew: I was going to be dismembered into a thousand pieces. My vehicle didn't have an airbag. My mind was exploding with a million thoughts about everything I cared for. It was all finished.

On the verge of certain death, one's brain goes through strange thoughts. Maybe I can write a whole book on the stream of thoughts that transpired. The Scorpio turtled on the road four times, came up straight, went to the shoulder and broke into pieces. I still held on to the steering. I checked my hands; they were intact. Pulled up my legs; they were also intact. I got down from the vehicle to see if my backbone was still there. No damage to it either. There was not one scratch on my body. Not one hair from my body was gone. My car didn't ram into any other car. It didn't even hit a pedestrian. How does one explain this? It was a sheer miracle. Thank God and Mahindra (makers of Scorpio). Thank God for the seat belt. I always wear them.

My family and friends were adamant that I should not drive any more. They concluded that I had lost my sense of coordination and that the accident happened because my reflexes were not fast enough. We had endless debate for days. I was not about to give up. I said that I will continue to drive. I love driving. I did promise I would slow down. I have stuck to my promise. Even prior to the accident, I would never violate a traffic rule. Even past midnight, I would halt at traffic lights. Now I am much more careful. It is not just about jumping traffic lights, half the guys out there on the road are crazy. They drive like lunatics. So I not only stick to the rule but also look around to make sure that someone is not going to ram into my car. I don't want to test God all the time demanding miracles.

I never let my wife or children drive without their driving license. In fact, my wife failed her first driving test when I was the district collector. I told the RTO that she should pass only when she was really good at it. Eventually, she became a competent driver and got her license.

When I was the union minister for tourism, I used to drive on Sundays to my office in my old Nissan Sunny alone. I needed time for myself, to think.

I turned seventy. I intend to drive for a long time. The moment I stop driving, I will grow old and die. But I owe it to myself, as a responsible citizen, to drive safely.

Everybody who gets behind the wheel must act responsibly. A vehicle in the hands of an irresponsible driver is a killer machine. While driving, concentrate only on the road. No mobile, no videos. Don't let your teenage kid, who doesn't have a driving license, get behind the wheels. If you do, you are wholly responsible for the consequences. Don't ever drive with liquor in your belly and brain.

> It is good to have passions but you need to know your and others' limits to stay safe.

Acknowledgements

When I retired from Parliament, my wife gave me a rather blunt piece of advice: 'Don't linger around the house and disturb the peace of my pets. Go out, come home to sleep, and if you arrive early, you will get dinner.' Given her deep commitment to animal activism, I knew exactly what she meant. So I made it a point to pack up my laptop after breakfast and head to the India International Centre (IIC) every single day, including Sundays. I made sure to return just in time for dinner. I owe a big thank you to Sheela for pulling me out of the post-retirement blues and nudging me to write this book.

This book is, in many ways, a product of the IIC. The atmosphere there, thanks to Ambassador Shyam Saran and Director K.N. Shrivastava, is incredible. If it weren't for the IIC library, I doubt whether this book would have come to life. I'm an orator at heart and not particularly fond of writing, but the library's ambiance compelled me to keep chipping away. My deepest gratitude goes to Usha Munshi, the gracious chief librarian, as well as Kanchan Nagpal, Puja Puri, Rajeev Mishra and the ever-smiling staff who made my time there so pleasant.

And let's not forget the food – without the delicious meals at the IIC, I'm not sure whether my brain would have functioned as well. A big thank you to the chefs and stewards at IIC. My lunchmates at the Lotus restaurant, Praveer Bagchi, R.K. Jain and Ashok Ogra, also deserve a shoutout for all the brainstorming sessions that helped shape the book's title.

I'm immensely grateful to Krishan Chopra, editor-in-chief at Bloomsbury, who persuaded me to take on this writing project. Krishan had previously edited my autobiography, *Making a Difference*, published by Penguin back in 1996 when I was just forty-two. The Malayalam translation, published by DC Books, became one of the bestselling non-fiction books in Malayalam. Krishan's cool demeanour and encouragement were invaluable.

Mekhala Moorthy, the editor of this book, has been a true professional. She took a nebulous idea and turned it into something beautiful. Without her, this book wouldn't have come to fruition.

Thanks to Krittika Gogoi, Chakrika Pandey and the editorial team at Bloomsbury for their work on the book.

A big thanks to Meenakshi Singh and the marketing team at Bloomsbury. You're the ones who will get people to read this book, and I'm counting on you.

My elder son, Akash, was a crucial sounding board for the book's conceptualisation. My younger son, Adarsh, and my daughter-in-law, Bridget, offered many valuable inputs that added spice to the book. Thank you all.

Finally, I appreciate Dr Shiekha John, a scientist with the Ministry of Earth Sciences, for her vital insights on global warming and the environment.

I am grateful to all those who read this book, because it is going to make the world happier.

Notes

Chapter 4: Mangaladevi: Where a God Was Threatened

1 Srikumar, A. 2015. 'Understanding Kannagi and Her Credo'. *The Hindu*, New Delhi, 19 February.

2 Pillai, S. 1982. 'Kerala and Tamil Nadu Spar Over Temple Dedicated to Goddess Kannagi'. *India Today*, 30 June.

Chapter 7: Golden Sheetal

1 *Indian Express*, 27 October 2023.

2 Modi, Narendra. X.Com. 27 October 2023.

3 Mahindra, Anand. X.Com. 28 October 2023.

4 *Times of India*, 25 October 2023.

5 *Times of India*, 25 October 2023.

Chapter 10: Blood vs Belief

1 Bijoe Emmanuel & Ors vs State Of Kerala & Ors (1986) 3 SCC 615

Chapter 11: With Them They Brought Light

1 *Indian Express*, 24 November 2023.

2 *Hindustan Times*, 30 November 2023.

3 *The Telegraph*, 30 November 2023.

4 Murmu, Draupadi. X.Com. 28 November 2023.

5 Modi, Narendra. X.Com. 28 November 2023.

6 Gadkari, Nitin. X.Com. 28 November 2023.

7 Mahindra, Anand. X.Com. 28 November 2023.

8 Ramesh, Jairam. X.Com. 28 November 2023.

Chapter 15: Sujatha and the Power of Self-Help Groups

1 *Down to Earth*. 8 March 2024.

2 Modi, Narendra. X.Com. 15 November 2024.

Chapter 22: You Are a Unique Creation

1 Craze, R. 2023. *The 7 Bad Habits of Highly Ineffective People*. New Holland Publishers.

Chapter 24: Sonam Wangchuk: The Snow Man

1 Hial.Edu.in.

2 *India Today*, 6 March 2020.

Chapter 25: Vasudhaiva Kutumbakam

1 Animal Welfare Board of India and Anr v. People for Elimination of Stray Troubles and Ors, Case No. CA 5988/2019 (Supreme Court of India)

Chapter 31: Dark Side of the Moon

1 Space News. 11 July 2023.

Chapter 32: The Quickgun Commissioner

1 Times of India. 2001. 'Bureaucrat Takes on Education Minister'. *Times of India*, 3 September.

Chapter 34: India: Global Digital Leader

1 *Economic Times*, 10 March 2024.

2 Budget Speech, 23 July 2024.

Chapter 35: Jadav Payeng: A Beacon of Hope for the Planet

1 Schueman, L.J. 2024. 'We Are Connected, the Wisdom of Jadav Payeng, India's Forest Man'. *One Earth*, 30 May.

About the Author

K.J. Alphons is from the 1979 batch of the Indian Administrative Service. He rose to national prominence as an effective administrator and anti-corruption crusader. He was the commissioner of the Delhi Development Authority and a pioneer of the literacy movement in India. The mass contact programme he started as a district collector won the highest UN award for innovation in governance. He was featured in the list of 100 Young Global Leaders by *Time* magazine. In 2006 Alphons left the civil service and joined politics. During his tenure as tourism minister, India was third in global tourism. He was also the minister of state for electronics and information technology. He is also a motivational speaker and the best-selling author of *Making a Difference*.